The Essential
Guardini

The Essential

Guardini

An Anthology of the Writings of

Romano Guardini

Selected and with an introduction by

Heinz R. Kuehn

LTP
LITURGY
TRAINING
PUBLICATIONS

Acknowledgments

All publication rights of Romano Guardini's works are jointly held by Matthias-Grünewald-Verlag, Mainz, and Verlag Ferdinand Schöningh, Paderborn. All author's rights are held by the Katholische Akademie in Bayerne, Munich. With permission.

Excerpts from the translations in this book are used with the permission of the copyright holders and are acknowledged on p. 181.

Copyright © 1997, Archdiocese of Chicago: Liturgy Training Publications, 1800 North Hermitage Avenue, Chicago IL 60622-1101; 1-800-933-1800; FAX 1-800-933-7094. All rights reserved.

This book was edited by Victoria M. Tufano. Audrey Novak Riley was the production editor. Mary E. Laur compiled the index. The book was designed by Anna Manhart, and Mark Hollopeter was the production artist. The typefaces used in this book are Slimbach and Fruitger. It was printed by Versa Press, Inc., East Peoria, Illinois.

Library of Congress Cataloging-in-Publications Data
Guardini, Romano, 1885 –1968
    The essential Guardini: an anthology of the writings of Romano Guardini/ selected and with an introduction by Heinz R. Kuehn.
      p. cm.
    Includes bibliographical references and index.
    ISBN 1-56854-133-3
    1. Catholic Church — Doctrines. 2. Catholic Church — Liturgy — Theology. 3. Church and the world — History of doctrines — 20th century. I. Kuehn, Heinz R. II. Title.
BX2705.G82A25 1997
230'.2 — dc21   97-8975
                                                                                            CIP

EGUARD

Contents

Introduction   1

Part 1
Our World   13

Chapter 1
Our World — Today and Tomorrow   14

The End of the Modern Age   14
Postmodernity and Democracy   15
Technology   16
The World Which Is to Come   18
The Unfolding of Power   18
The New Culture: Danger   26
The New Life: Cosmic Interdependence   28
Building the Emerging World   32
Possibilities of Action   36
The Task   43

Chapter 2
Our Life — Today and Tomorrow   50

Anxiety   50
Nature   51
Destroy or Build?   51
Demons   52
Personality   53
Chaos   54
The Stakes   55
Solitude   55
Love   57
Values   58
Grace   62

Part 2
Jesus Christ 65

Chapter 3
The Message of Salvation 66

Mystery and Revelation 66
Belief in Christ 70
The Beatitudes 76
Mysterium Fidei 79

Chapter 4
Faith and Doubt 85

God's Patience 85
Faith and Doubt in the Stages of Life 89
Adoration 93

Part 3
The Church 97

Chapter 5
The Birth of the Church 98

The Scriptural Testimony 98
Pentecost: The Event 103
Pentecost: The Consequences 108
Christ Is the Church 113

Chapter 6
We Are the Church 116

The People of God 116
Christ Bound Himself 117
Contemporaneity with Jesus Christ 119
Church, Personality and Community 120

Part 4
Liturgy and Worship   131

Chapter 7
Congregation, Fellowship and Prayer   132

The Congregation and the Church   132
The Fellowship of the Liturgy   136
The Prayer of the Liturgy   140

Chapter 8
Liturgy: Playful and Serious   147

The Playfulness of the Liturgy   147
The Seriousness of the Liturgy   152

Chapter 9
Sacred Signs   155

The Symbolism of the Liturgy   157
The Altar as Table   157
The Sign of the Cross   160
The Hands   161
Standing   163
Doors   164
Candles   165
Holy Water   167
Bread and Wine   168
Blessing   170
Time Sanctified   171
The Name of God   175

Selected Bibliography   178
  Works by Guardini in English Translation   178
  Works about Guardini and Related Works   179
  Works Excerpted in This Volume   181
Index   182

Introduction

When Liturgy Training Publications (LTP) asked me to compile for publication an anthology of Romano Guardini's most important writings, I had to ask myself whether I was the right person to accept the assignment. My hesitation was based on the following considerations: To most American Catholics, Guardini is known by his book *The Lord* and, it seems, to a lesser degree by his works about the liturgy and the church, such as *Sacred Signs, The Spirit of the Liturgy, The Church and the Catholic* and *Meditations Before Mass*. To most people born after the Second World War, even the name of Romano Guardini seems largely unknown. Moreover, the mission statement of LTP states explicitly that it "is to provide materials that assist parishes, institutions and households in the preparation, celebration and expression of liturgy in Christian life."

As important as the above-mentioned books are to an understanding of Guardini and his influence on the church and its liturgy, to me they reflect only part of what I and many Europeans see in him. I grew up in Berlin during the Weimar Republic, lived and worked during the Nazi regime as a half-Jew under Gestapo supervision and became a writer on Catholic themes after the Second World War. From the time I converted to Catholicism in 1934, at the age of 14, until I immigrated to the United States in 1951, Guardini was one of my most influential spiritual, intellectual and cultural guides — and so he remains to this day. I see in him one of those rare Catholic thinkers who, like many of the Catholic novelists of his and my generation, had a truly cosmic view of Catholicism and life's realities. To assemble an anthology that represented what might be called "the essential Guardini," I had to include books that were devoted to a critique and analysis of the modern age in all its aspects and which, even though they had been translated into English, had become in this country a virtually forgotten legacy. When I explained to LTP that, in my opinion, to assemble a true anthology of Guardini's writing I had to include texts from these books because they in large part remain as relevant for today as for the time when they were written, LTP readily agreed.

For these reasons it may be useful at this point to offer a brief biography of Guardini, particularly since I am one of the few surviving members of my generation who had the unforgettable experience of having known Guardini personally. That alone, I hope, will elevate this sketch above the dryness of an encyclopedia entry and help to bring the man and his work to life.

Romano Guardini was born on February 17, 1885, in Verona, one of Italy's most fascinating cultural centers. His father was an importer of eggs and poultry. When Romano was one year old, the family, including three sons, moved to Mainz, Germany, situated on the confluence of the Main and Rhine Rivers, a city whose origins go back to early Roman times. His childhood, as he tells in *Berichte über mein Leben*,[1] was an unhappy one. His mother kept the children virtually captive in their home, which made it difficult for them to socialize with neighborhood children and classmates.

His youth was a time of inner tumult, uncertainty about his vocation and painful attacks of depression. In 1903 the shy and melancholy Guardini graduated from the gymnasium (a classical preparatory school for the university) in Mainz and the same year began the study of chemistry at the University of Tübingen. Depressed and lonely, he left the university after two semesters and in 1904 enrolled at the University of Munich for the study of economics, which he continued the following year at the University of Berlin.

That year, 1905, he had a deep crisis of faith from which he eventually emerged with the decision to study theology. Yet his inner turmoil subsided for only a brief time. In 1906 he began his theological studies in Freiburg im Breisgau but depression again took hold, to such a degree that he considered suicide. Still, he stuck to his decision, and from then on he knew that the priesthood was his only and true vocation.

He continued his theological studies in Tübingen in 1906 and 1907. During that time he had his first exposure to true liturgy when he visited the Abbey of Beuron, whose monks were among the early pioneers of liturgical renewal. Liturgy from then on became for him a prime and lifelong interest.

In 1908 he entered the seminary in Mainz; he was ordained in 1910, the year his father became the Italian consul in that city. Guardini's propensity for critical dialogue with contemporary ideas was looked on by his teachers with suspicion, and his ordination had been postponed by half a year. The suspicion of adherence to

Modernism, the philosophical-theological movement to adapt the teaching of religion and its practice to the results of modern science and the needs of the modern person, was still in the air. For Guardini, who once said that "the church does not restrict freedom but, on the contrary, gives complete freedom toward the totality of being,"[2] it was a disappointingly unhappy time.

The next 13 years, between 1910 and 1923, were not only busy and, in many ways, unsatisfactory for him, but also a period during which he eventually came into his own. He served as associate pastor in Heppenheim, Darmstadt, Worms and Mainz, cities whose evidence of their Roman and medieval past inspired and consoled him, lifting him out of depression and beyond uncertainties in his search for his true calling. During this period he also acquired German citizenship (1911), continued his theological studies in Freiburg and received his doctorate in theology with a dissertation on the teaching of Saint Bonaventure on salvation. Summarizing his experience of pastoral ministry during these years of searching, he observes:

> I must say that I did not find the human relationship which the pastor must have with his congregation. Still, I was also convinced that pastoral ministry was the proper form of priesthood. Yet, I have never found my way to the people, to the way they think and to the forms of their interests. . . . Rather — without starting out from this or that principle but simply from my spontaneous attitude toward pastoral tasks — I found myself the type of brotherly priest who does not act out of his official position but carries the priesthood in himself as a pastoral force; who does not confront the faithful as the owner of authority but stands next to them. He is reluctant to offer them firm results and directions but joins them in their searching and asking in order to arrive with them at common results.[3]

In 1915 Guardini's family left Germany because of the war; they returned in 1919, but his father died soon thereafter and the family again settled in Italy. From 1916 to 1918 Guardini served in the military as a hospital orderly, but at the same time, from 1915 to 1920, he also directed Juventus, a Catholic organization of students of higher education in whose company he found his ideal way of being involved in pastoral ministry.

In many ways, his work with Juventus was a precursor to his later involvement in the Quickborn movement. Youth movements flourished in Germany from the beginning of the twentieth century until they were suppressed by the Nazis or incorporated into the Hitler Youth. Helmut Kuhn describes the driving forces of these movements:

> The German youth movement in the beginning of the twentieth century rebelled against the world of the adults — against their untrustworthy conventions, their superficial amusements, against orders unjustified by any true authority, against a sexual morality that confused external civility with purity and who hid their helplessness behind a deliberate attitude of ignorance, and against the urbanization of an existence alienated from nature. This world of adulthood and middle-class mentality which they viewed as hostile, the young rebels did not know how to counter with a faith or a philosophy, let alone a program, but only (and that was not little) with their youth and the exuberance it generated. . . . What was at stake for them was the acquisition or restitution of true relationships between person and person beyond the barriers of class and gender. These wandering singers of songs wanted to be poor so that they could be companions; they scorned bourgeois comforts so that they could join in living the beauty of their youth among the joys and burdens of the open sky.
>
> Guardini the educator let himself be seized by the mental and spiritual beauty of this youth and at the same time recognized the danger to which they were exposed: the threatened waste of their energy in an anarchic effort and, consequently, their vulnerability to intellectual seduction and incapacity to find their way back into the life of active adulthood. Out of love and sorrow the thought arose in him to subject this fermenting youth to the holy discipline of the church, not in order to gag their freedom but to save them — to show these young people who so resolutely rebelled against "the old" (yet which was a rather modern "old") the never-aging youth of the oldest truths.[4]

When Guardini was still associate pastor in Mainz, another encounter in 1916 was equally decisive in helping him to arrive at the inner security and maturity for which the 30-year-old had by now been searching for more than 15 years: his acquaintance and later friendship with Ildefons Herwegen, abbot of the Benedictine monastery of Maria Laach, which had become the center for liturgical renewal in Germany. The abbey was considering the publication of a series of monographs, *Ecclesia Orans,* dealing with things liturgical, and when Guardini showed the abbot a manuscript containing lectures he had given in Mainz, the abbot was so impressed by it that it became the first in the series under the title "Vom Geist der Liturgie" (The Spirit of the Liturgy). It appeared as a book in 1918 and immediately became a best-seller in Germany and beyond. At the suggestion of Abbot Herwegen, who wanted him to join the Catholic theological faculty at the University of Bonn, Guardini wrote a habilitation (a thesis required of candidates wishing to lecture at a university) about Saint Bonaventure's teaching on the illumination of the mind, and subsequently received a position as lecturer in dogmatics at the University of Bonn in 1922.

At that time the University of Berlin was searching for someone qualified to assume a newly founded chair of Philosophy of Religion and Catholic *Weltanschauung* (worldview), a position established at the insistence of the politically influential Catholic Center Party. The university was considered Germany's stronghold of Protestantism, and its faculty therefore was vigorously opposed to the inclusion of such a chair among its faculty. A compromise was eventually reached by incorporating that chair into the Department of Theology of the University of Breslau and entitling its possessor in Berlin "permanent guest professor." When Guardini was offered this guest professorship, he was at first reluctant but after much thought and consultation with friends accepted it. He moved to Berlin in 1923, the same year his book *The Church and the Catholic* appeared.

In Berlin he found himself in an awkward and often embarrassing position. Shunned by the faculty and holding a chair unadvertised to the students, he felt like a stranger in a place where for the first time he was able to bring his knowledge and experience into full play. But his reputation as a teacher spread rapidly, and it was not long before his lecture hall was filled to capacity not only by students but also by professors of other faculties and by members of Berlin's Catholic intellectual elite. He had, in short, come into his own.

The city that would become Guardini's home for 20 years had nothing in common with the orderly and peaceful places in which he had lived, studied and worked until now. It seemed as if all the bloody turmoil that characterized the Weimar Republic, Germany's first experiment with democracy, was centered in its capital. At an international conference on Romano Guardini held at Notre Dame University in the fall of 1994, I described the Germany of that day:

> Germany was reeling under the crushing burden of the Treaty of Versailles, which had imposed on it hundreds of billions of dollars in war reparations, had split off one-eighth of its territory with a population of seven million and had given to France for 15 years its most productive industrial region, the Saarland. Equally disastrous, the governing coalition was under relentless attack from the radical left — the Communists and the radical Socialists — and from the radical right — the ultranationalists and the National Socialists, the Nazis. More important for our theme, the war had dealt a devastating blow to a western world that still rested on an essentially Christian framework of values and ushered in the era of nihilism, existentialism and relativism.[5]

In addition, there were food riots, pitched street battles among scores of political parties, assassinations of leading political figures, rising unemployment and inflation. In the year Guardini arrived in Berlin, Hitler attempted a coup in Munich to bring the city under his control. Upon its failure, he was imprisoned in the fortress of Landsberg where he wrote his infamous *Mein Kampf* ("My Fight") in which he articulated his program for a Germany under Nazi dictatorship.

The difficulty for Guardini was to develop themes for his lectures that would be meaningful for an audience living under these conditions. His advantage was that the Catholic church, because of the powerful political influence of the Center Party, flourished. Moreover, Berlin under the Weimar Republic had become the cultural center of Europe in art, music, theater, the cinema and literature, giving him points of contact for his lectures that corresponded to his own interest in the arts. After some experimentation he focused his themes on the main issues of Christian ethics and the New Testament, and gradually turned to the Christian interpretation of literary masterpieces by writers such as Saint Augustine, Dante, Kierkegaard, Pascal and Hölderlin. He amplified his lectures at the university with lectures and workshops before different audiences at such places as the Jesuit church of Saint Canisius. Whatever time he could spare he spent directing the Catholic youth movement Quickborn ("Fountain of Youth"), whose headquarters was the medieval castle of Rothenfels on the river Main; he also served as editor of the movement's journal *Schildgenossen* ("Comrades of the Shield"), a national Catholic periodical devoted to theological, liturgical and cultural subjects.

Rothenfels became one of the few places where Guardini felt truly at home. He "insisted that the Quickborn promote the cultural life of youth as well as their spiritual and social dimensions," writes Robert Krieg.

> As a result, at the Quickborn's local and national gatherings young people discussed theater, art and literature, played musical instruments and joined in retreats and pilgrimages to holy shrines. At Burg Rothenfels young men and women from all corners of Germany learned folk dances and folk songs, acted in the plays of Shakespeare and even performed puppet shows. They also participated in informal Masses at which they sang hymns in German instead of Latin, discussed the scriptural readings for the day and stood around the altar at which the priest faced the people. Further, they were introduced to Guardini's vision of a "new Europe" that would transcend national and ethnic boundaries and be founded on the West's tradition of humanism.[6]

My first personal encounter with Guardini occurred in the fall of 1938 at the Students' Chapel, Saint Benedict, in Berlin Charlottenburg where Guardini customarily celebrated the Sunday Mass. I was 19 years old and lived in the Catholic Students' Home a short distance from the chapel. In the same address from which I quoted earlier, I summarized my encounter with Guardini in the chapel:

> The chapel was a small, unadorned room located in the semi-basement of an apartment building. It had a few rows of chairs, a small, table-like, free-standing altar, and the only natural light came from a couple of oblong windows under its ceiling on the level of the street. . . . If I wanted to explain in a few words what drew me and the small congregation that came from all parts of Berlin to Guardini's Mass, it was simply this: He was a person who by his words and actions drew us into a world where the sacred became convincingly and literally tangible. His mere appearance radiated something for which I have no better word than *luminous;* in his presence one fell silent and became all attention. With him on the altar, the sacred table became the center of the universe. But was it a universe of fantasy? Of

escape? Of religious sentiment that did not survive for 24 hours? Or was it the center of *our* universe, *our* daily reality? . . . And yet for us, we found the foothold that gave us the strength and courage to face, to endure and to resist a world in which the forces of evil, Satan and his demons, were running rampant, in that small chapel in the presence of a man whose words and actions made truth appear to us as a physical presence. The impact of the sacred action was all the more profound because Guardini celebrated the Mass *versus populum* — facing the people. It was a *missa recitata,* a Mass at which people responded aloud to the presider's prayers, something still new in those days, and we, the congregation, were the altar boys and girls answering his invitations to prayer.

In his *Berichte über mein Leben,* which appeared posthumously, Guardini himself specifically refers to the Saint Benedict Chapel: "What I wanted to do (in the chapel) from the very beginning, first instinctively, then more and more consciously, was this: to make the truth glow. Truth is a power, provided you don't demand an immediate effect, but rather have patience and expect that it will take a long time (before you see results). . . . If anywhere, then here, lack of purpose is the greatest power. I have often had that experience. Sometimes, especially in the last years, I had a sense that the truth was standing in space like a living body."[7]

I learned only much later that Guardini's homilies in the chapel were to serve as the first draft of his most popular book, *The Lord.* It doesn't matter, either, that I found him unapproachable, even abrupt in social encounters, somewhat shy and unwilling to be drawn into anything resembling mere chitchat. What matters is that during those 30 or 40 minutes he gave us the sustenance that nourished us for another week of uncertainty, danger and fear, the strength to face Satan and his demons for another week, and that a mere evocation of his presence at the altar and of his words brought light even into our darkest moments of hopelessness or despair.

In 1939 the Nazis dismissed Guardini from the university, dissolved the Quickborn movement and closed its headquarters, Burg Rothenfels. He stayed in Berlin for another four years, writing and giving workshops before various Catholic audiences. Some of his most important, popular and enduring books were published during his Berlin years, such as *The Church and the Catholic* (1923),

Letters from Lake Como (1927), *Sacred Signs* (1929), *The Lord* (1937), *The World and the Person* (1939) and *Meditations Before Mass* (1939), among others. There is no doubt that the bloody upheavals of the time of the Weimar Republic and the subsequent Nazi regime, as well as the renaissance of the Catholic church that began to stir after the First World War, were decisive for his choice of themes and gave his writings the depth and richness of his reflections and the persuasive force of his mental appeal. He became a household word for literate Catholics (as well as for many adherents of other denominations) and remained, if you will, ubiquitous until after his death.

When the air raids on Berlin turned the city into a vast field of rubble and ruins, he left it in 1943 and moved to Mooshausen in rural southern Germany, where he lived with his lifelong friend Pastor Josef Weiger and wrote his autobiographical reflections, *Berichte über mein Leben.*

My last personal encounter with Romano Guardini occurred at the University of Tübingen, where he had assumed the chair of Philosophy of Religion and Christian *Weltanschauung* after the war had ended in 1945, and where I enrolled in 1947 to study philosophy, history and religion. Here I had the same experience I had in Berlin when I attended — secretly, as a half-Jew under Gestapo supervision — his lectures at that city's university. Although his innate shyness kept him from being a good speaker, and although he tended to overreact to the slightest disturbance in the lecture hall, he attracted an overflowing audience of students and faculty of virtually all disciplines. The secret of his popularity was simple: Here was a man who, after Europe's bloodiest and most turbulent era, penetrated in his lectures to the essence of a truly Christian vision of the world. He did not lecture in terms of abstract theological or philosophical principles but in terms of the stark and often violent realities of our world, connecting them with the traditions of the western world in religion, art, literature and architecture, and persuasively demonstrating the life-giving validity of the old, yet ever-young, verities of Christianity for a generation trying to come to terms with the Second World War and its consequences.

In 1948, the year I left Tübingen to begin a career as a freelance writer in Berlin, Guardini accepted the specially created chair of Professor of Philosophy of Religion and Christian *Weltanschauung* at the University of Munich and remained in this position until 1963, when he was succeeded by Karl Rahner. For this introduction, suffice it to say that he remained as active, influential and popular in his lectures and as prolific in his writings as he had been during his years in Berlin and Tübingen. In addition, he preached every Sunday during the academic year to an overflowing congregation at the university's Saint Ludwig Church. It was during his Munich years that he wrote, among other books, *The End of the Modern World* (1950), *Power and Responsibility* (1951) and *The Church of the Lord* (1965), books from which excerpts have been selected for this anthology.

By the time Guardini died in 1968 at the age of 83, he had written at least 60 books and 100 articles, an output the Catholic Academy in Bavaria is now assembling and publishing as Guardini's collected works. In addition, he had preached and lectured to thousands of listeners, and through his written and spoken word made a profound impact on Catholics around the world. He has been called many names — a Renaissance man, a precursor of Vatican II, a lighthouse in a darkening world, a prophet of things to come, a humanistic scholar in the best sense of the word — characterizations that remain valid to this day. He received numerous public honors, including the coveted Erasmus Prize, and near the end of his life was even offered the cardinal's hat, which he refused. His influence and popularity in Europe and the United States waned during the turbulent '60s and '70s, but has now been revived to an astonishing degree.

Some of Guardini's observations and reflections are, of course, outdated, particularly in view of the developments in the church after Vatican II. However, by far the greatest part of his work is as pertinent today as it was when he wrote it. It is, indeed, prophetic in the sense that he foresaw decades ago the destructive as well as the positive elements in the modern or, if you will, postmodern age, and their consequences for the life of the church and its individual members. This prophetic element in Guardini's writings and the orientation they give to contemporary men and women was for me a determining factor in the selection of the texts presented in this anthology.

The Texts in This Book

All of the books from which excerpts were selected have appeared in English translation. Each excerpt in this book is accompanied by the English title of the work from which it was taken, and the page numbers from the English edition listed in the bibliography at the end of this book. The date of the book's first publication in German follows in parentheses. Since they most impressively reflected the "essential Guardini," and since the translations were uniformly good, there was no need to translate them again from the original German for this anthology. However, all of them were translated, as was the practice of the time, using "man" and male pronouns as generic terms for men and women, something particularly noticeable in Guardini's works because his focus is on the human person. From this point of departure he develops all of his themes, whether they concern religion, politics, history or liturgy. In German, the generic word for the human person is *Mensch*, which denotes both man and woman, and the words denoting the specific gender of man and woman are *Mann* and *Frau*. We can't make that distinction in English because, even though the word "man," the accurate translation of the word *Mensch*, was once understood to denote both men and women, it is no longer understood so. Liturgy Training Publications therefore asked the various original publishers for permission to change the language of their translations slightly to suit the contemporary sensibility regarding the inclusion of women in language. Some publishers permitted us to adapt the texts; others did not.

Moreover, wherever permission was given to use inclusive language, any words that appeared in the British spelling were Americanized. Finally, scriptural quotations, which were taken from different Bible editions in different texts, were left unchanged.

Although all of this affected to some degree the uniformity of the anthology's style, Guardini's world of thought and the depth, richness and beauty of his imagery speak to us as eloquently and persuasively today as they did when his books first appeared, and will prove to be so irresistible that the reader will almost immediately become oblivious to any stylistic inconsistency in the chosen texts.

Heinz R. Kuehn

1. Romano Guardini. *Berichte über mein Leben* ("Reports about My Life"). Düsseldorf: Patmos Verlag, 1984, 58 ff., 61. All quotations from *Berichte über mein Leben* are translations by Heinz R. Kuehn.

2. Ibid., 36.

3. Ibid., 98–99.

4. Helmut Kuhn. *Romano Guardini. Der Mensch und das Werk* ("Romano Guardini. The Man and the Work"). Munich: Kösel-Verlag, no date, 29–31. Translated by Heinz R. Kuehn.

5. Heinz R. Kuehn. "Fires in the Night: Germany 1920–1950" in *Romano Guardini: Proclaiming the Sacred in a Modern World.* Ed. Robert Krieg, csc. Chicago: Liturgy Training Publications, 1995, 2.

6. Robert A. Krieg, csc. "A Precursor's Life and Work" in *Romano Guardini: Proclaiming the Sacred in a Modern World.* 23.

7. Romano Guardini. *Berichte über mein Leben.* 109–110.

Part 1

Our World

Chapter 1

Our World — Today and Tomorrow

In all crucial respects the modern world has come to an end. Since the spirit of an age becomes wholly clear only when it has begun to vanish from the face of the earth, it has been possible to draw a picture of the modern world without falling victim either in a spirit of admiration or of hatred to the thing represented.

The End of the Modern World, page 15 (German publication: 1955)

The End of the Modern Age

Today the modern age is essentially over. The chains of cause and effect that it established will of course continue to hold. Historical epochs are not neatly severed like the steps of a laboratory experiment. While one era prevails, its successor is already forming, and its predecessor continues to exert influence for a long time. To this day we find elements of a still-vital antiquity in southern Europe, and we run across strong medieval currents in many places. Thus in the yet nameless epoch which we feel breaking in on us from all sides, the last consequences of the modern age are still being drawn, although that which determined the essence of that age no longer determines the character of the historical epoch now beginning.

Everywhere man's power is in unbroken ascendancy. Indeed, we might contend that his power has only now entered upon its critical stage. Nevertheless, essentially, the will of the age is no longer directed to the augmenting of power as such. The modern age considered every increase in intellectual-technical power an unquestionable gain, fervently believing all such increase to be progress, progress in the direction of a decisive fulfillment of the supreme meaning and value of existence. Today this belief is growing shaky, a condition which in itself indicates the beginning of a new epoch. We no longer believe that increase of power is necessarily the same thing as increase of value. Power has grown questionable. And not merely from the standpoint of a cultural critique (like that which opposed the prevailing optimism of the nineteenth century, especially toward its end) but fundamentally questionable. Into the public consciousness creeps the suspicion that our whole attitude toward power is wrong; more, that our growing power is a growing threat to ourselves. That threat finds its expression in the nuclear bomb, which has captured the vital awareness and imagination of the public and become the symbol of something fraught with more general meaning.

In the coming epoch, the essential problem will no longer be that of increasing power — though power will continue to increase at an ever swifter tempo — but of curbing it. The core of the new epoch's intellectual task will be to integrate power into life in such a way that man can employ power without forfeiting his humanity. For he will have only two choices: to match the greatness of his power with the strength of his humanity, or to surrender his humanity to power and perish. The very fact that we can define these alternatives without seeming utopian or moralistic — because by so doing we but voice something of which the public is more or less aware — is further indication that the new epoch is overtaking the old.

Power and Responsibility, pages xii – xiii (1955)

Postmodernity and Democracy

If we do not read the history of the past hundred years as a process of decay, then what positive meaning does it have? It is found without doubt in the value achieved by men and women as they shoulder the work of dominating their world. That work will make such tremendous demands of people that they could never achieve it by individual initiative or even by the united effort of individuals bred to an individualistic way. The work of dominating the world calls for a union of skills and a unity of achievement that can only grow from quite a different attitude. This new attitude is revealed by the evident fact that the coming human persons renounce an idiosyncratic life for a communal form, that they surrender individual initiative for a given order of things. The process of conformity has profaned so many areas of life and has done so much violence to people that we are apt to neglect its positive meaning, a meaning which it does possess. It lies behind the immensity of the work to be done; it lies in the corresponding greatness of an individual's position facing a given task, in a person's solidarity with it, in his or her comradeship for co-workers. When all other substantial values have disintegrated, comradeship remains. This fact can and ought to be understood, I think, as a sign of what is to come. The new comradeship will be comradeship in the task of preserving being itself, a comradeship in the work of facing future danger and menace. If this comradeship is accepted in accord with the true meaning of "person," it will be the supreme human value to come from the great body of the common people. Even under the changing conditions brought by that body, comradeship could help to regain the values of the "person": benevolence, understanding and justice.

These considerations force us to conclude that democratic values, as much as they are reiterated, demand careful and sober reflection. The crisis which confronts democracy has arisen because it received its historical imprint from the attitudes of a personality culture. Thus democratic values presumed a small population. It is evident that a genuine democratic spirit, in that sense, is only possible in small countries or in the large country which possesses great spaces of open land. The effectiveness of democratic values for the new age is problematic. Can they be reintegrated by the person facing the meager and stark conditions of human life as it will be lived in the future? Can they revitalize that person in his or her life within the great body of the common people?

The End of the Modern World, pages 84, 85 (1955)

Technology

The world outlook now being born or, precisely, the tendencies within that outlook, refuse to venerate nature. . . . This shifting relationship manifests itself even as it leaves itself undefined in the striking complex of knowledge, theory, skill and mode of production summed up in the term "technics," that is, in technology. During the nineteenth century, technology developed slowly; for that stretch of time it developed only at the hands of a non-technological mentality. Then at last in the decades just prior to World War II, and in the years of that war, the individual motivated by technology broke into the field of history and took possession. This technological individual experiences nature neither as a standard of value nor as a living shelter for his or her spirit.

The technological mind sees nature as an insensate order, as a cold body of facts, as a mere given, as an object of utility, as raw material to be hammered into useful shape; it views the cosmos similarly as a mere space into which objects can be thrown with complete indifference. Technological individuals will remold the world; they see their task as Promethean and its stakes as being and non-being.

The modern era was fond of justifying technology and rested its defense upon the argument that technology promoted the well-being of humanity. In doing so it masked the destructive effects of a ruthless system. I do not believe that the age to come will rest with such an argument. The person engaged today in the labor of "technics" knows full well that technology moves forward in final analysis neither for profit nor for the well-being of the race. That person knows in the most radical sense of the term that power is its motive — a lordship of all; that person seizes the naked elements of both nature and human nature. His or her action bespeaks immense possibilities not only for creation but also for destruction, especially for the destruction of humanity itself. People as human beings are far less rooted and fixed within their own essence than is commonly accepted. This terrible danger grows day by day. Once the autonomous state has broken all bonds, it will be able to deliver the last *coup de grâce* to human nature itself. The relationship of the human being with nature has reached the point of final crisis: people will either succeed in converting their mastery into good — then their accomplishment would be immense indeed — people will either do that, or they themselves will be at an end.

Within this area of choice an emotion partaking of the religious seems to penetrate again. This religious feeling . . . is bound up intrinsically with the dangers for the people and for their earth which they have found locked up with their technological power. The new religious emotion wells up from a sense of the profound loneliness which a person knows in the midst of all that is now summed up by the term "the world"; people's emotions grow out of the realization that as they approach their ultimate decision they must face it with responsibility, with resolution and with bravery.

The End of the Modern World, pages 73, 74, 75 (1950)

The World Which Is to Come

The intellectual consciousness of modern Europe as commonly delineated and accepted even in our day proclaimed these three ideals: a nature subsisting in itself, an autonomous personality of the human subject and a culture self-created out of norms intrinsic to its own essence. The European mind believed further that the constant creation and perfection of this culture constituted the final goal of history. This was all a mistake. Of the many signs appearing today, all point to the fact that these cherished ideals are fading from history.

My hypothesis has nothing in common, however, with that cheap disposition which revels always in prophesying collapse or destruction. It has nothing in common with that desire which would surrender the valid achievements of modern humankind. Nor is my hypothesis linked with a longing for a romantically envisioned Middle Ages or with an advance into a glorified utopia of the future. But this hypothesis has its crucial importance; it will enable us both to understand and to master the meanings implicit to the new world that is upon us. That humanity was matured and deepened by its experience of the modern world cannot be denied. This truth is self-evident despite the ominous spectacle of a human nature withering beneath the destructive hand of modernity.

Our concern of the moment is neither to repudiate nor to glorify; it is to understand the modern world, to comprehend why it is coming to an end. We seek to apprehend the nature of the world epoch which is being born out of the womb of history. As yet history has not named its offspring.

The End of the Modern World, pages 68, 69 (1950)

The Unfolding of Power

The transformation of process and product is accompanied by a corresponding change in the working man himself. The handicrafts, on which all preceding culture was based, are disappearing. As the machine is perfected, the intimate relation of man to his work, in which his eye, hand, will, sense of material, imagination and general creativeness cooperate, disappears. Process and product alike become ever further removed from intellectual-physical norms and forces. They are founded on scientific knowledge and the practicalities of construction, and effected by mechanical processes.

As a result, in some respects, man himself grows poorer. He loses the rich satisfaction of personal creativity, consenting instead to invent, utilize and service mechanical contraptions. But even as he puts them to ever more varied tasks, gaining through them ever greater power, his own will and creativeness must conform ever more to the mechanism in question, for one-sided effects do not exist. This means that the producer renounces individuality in his product and learns to content himself with producing only what the machine allows. The more perfect the apparatus, the fewer the possibilities of personal creativeness. And along with diminishing creativity, the human element, which lives so strongly in work made by hand, is also lost. In place of the artisan we have the worker, servicer of machines. For the customer too, something is lost, the personal contact with things that is possible only between persons and personally created objects. The customer is reduced to the modern consumer whose tastes are dictated by mass production, advertising and sales techniques. And this to the point where he comes to consider the standards and values which only genuine craftsmanship can satisfy as senseless or effete.

If nature is being more and more subjected to the control of man and his works, man himself is also increasingly controlled by those who fit him into "the system," even as his work is controlled by the end to which it is directed. Moreover, the consumer — in other words, everyone — now lives in a world of consumer goods, and hence in turn is constantly subjected to their influence.

Non-human Humanity

Indeed, the consequences reach still further. The culture which preceded technology's full breakthrough was characterized by the fact that man could experience personally what he theoretically perceived and physically created. Knowledge and creative possibility on the one hand, personal experience on the other, tallied in a measure which determined his whole attitude. From this blossomed that strikingly organic harmony so typical of pretechnical culture. Today the possibilities of knowing and doing progressively outstrip those of experiencing. The result is a world of thought, action and works that are no longer capable of being experienced — a world that man has come to consider as an objective process complete in itself.

In [*The End of the Modern World,*] I suggested the term "non-human humanity" to describe the kind of human beings that are both the condition and the result of this process. Here I can only repeat: I know how misleading the expression is, but I am unable to find one better. It does not mean the inhuman being who, as a glance at history will prove, was possible also in the "human" epoch. It means man in whom the earlier relative agreement between the fields of knowledge and works on the one hand, and of experience on the other, is no longer found. He exists in a world of knowledge-works possibilities that have outstripped earlier norms. (Let us take an example. If a man attacks and kills another with a club, he experiences his act directly. It is quite another thing when he pulls a lever in an airplane at high altitude, and hundreds of thousands perish in cities far below him. He is capable of knowing and causing such an act; he is no longer capable of experiencing it as an act and event. In various ways this is true also for much else in contemporary life.)

Closely related to this, its cause and its result, is one of the most universal and most disturbing symptoms of the shift in the human condition that we have: the matter-of-factness of the new man. In a way, this matter-of-factness demonstrates modern man's will and ability to concentrate on the task at hand regardless of personal feelings, on tasks that are becoming increasingly great and demanding; it demonstrates further his unwillingness, standing as he does ever more plainly in the public eye, to display emotions of any kind, indeed, even to harbor them. But it also evinces a growing inability to see, a progressive cooling of the heart, an indifference to the people and things of existence. A common substitute for genuine feeling is sensation, that superficial ersatz emotion excitement — which, though momentarily strong, is neither fruitful nor lasting.

. . . What has been said so far could be interpreted as a description of humanity's decline. A large segment of current opinion actually does so interpret the historical process now unfolding. I beg to disagree.

The person who takes this stand, usually unconsciously of course, identifies the universally human with the humanity of a particular, though long, historical period. The number and variety of its phenomena mislead him; still more does the fact that his own cultural roots are nourished by it. Thus he is prone to certain false conclusions. For one thing, he overlooks the negative possibilities that existed also in the past. Not without reason did we consider the theological aspects of power before the philosophical. Man's inner confusion as described by Revelation is characteristic, not of any one epoch but of all. It is part of fallen mankind. Naturally, from a Christian point of view, it is decline when the modern age as a whole draws away from Revelation, and it is understandable that the Christian interpretation of history dwells affectionately on the Middle Ages. However, it should not be forgotten that direct application of the truths of Revelation to world problems also has its dark side. The fact is too readily overlooked that Christian truths are by no means self-evident and that they speak of judgment as well as grace. Hence both their correct interpretation and their practical application presuppose a constant *metanoia*, or conversion. Where this is absent, we have a pseudo-Christianity which leaves life's real substance untouched.

Considered thus, the pretechnical epochs also embraced all the possibilities of injustice and destruction, but they operated within a psychological climate whose basic organic harmony made them appear less harmful than they would be later. Seen in this larger view, the dangers which began to be evident in the modern age, and which are becoming ever more pressing, are but the revelation of possibilities which have existed in all ages.

What Is Human?

To touch bottom, when we set up "the human" as a norm, what do we mean? We can mean the essence of all possibilities that exist in man: his various attitudes to the world, the tasks he faces and the achievements which are his response to them. But people who feel more at home in the past than in the present are inclined to limit these many human possibilities to those which dominated history up to a certain point, be it the end of the Middle Ages, the beginning of modern times, the close of the early Victorian era or the outbreak of World War I. Moreover, they are prone to consider the norms of their favorite epoch the sole guarantors of a sound, dignified human existence. Thus later developments are necessarily regarded as a decline from the essentially human — especially in certain circles devoted to a humanistic point of view.

But whenever this happens, the concept "man" is being considered far too narrowly. For an essentially human characteristic is man's ability to cross the bounds of the organic-harmonious without becoming less "human" than he was before. Naturally, at such times the dangers we described come to the fore more strongly, more unambiguously than ever, so that, historically speaking, man does face the real and apparent crisis of his humanity. But "crisis" always means choice between positive and negative possibilities, and the real question is which way man's decision is to fall. If in the present crisis the dangers of the negative choice of injustice and destruction seem greater than ever before, only the intensity of those dangers is new, nothing essential, for these have always existed in man, not exclusively in the man of the future. All we can do is accept the present situation and, strengthened by the purest powers of the mind and of grace, overcome these dangers from within. Should we fail, it would not be because our epoch as such is declining and falling; in all epochs man is in a state of decline and fall and in need of redemption — only in certain periods, under certain conditions, this fact can be concealed more easily than in others.

The above certainly does not mean that we should simply assent to whatever occurs today and will occur tomorrow. It is only a protest against the practice of identifying humanity as such, and of laying the possibilities of destruction, so glaringly evident today, solely at the feet of the new epoch. That would be the kind of pessimism that insures defeat from the start.

But let us return to our subject. The dissolution of organic creativity finds a counterpart in the dissolution of the basic unit of mature human life. The family is losing its significance as an integrating, order-preserving factor. Congregation, city, country are being influenced less and less by the family, clan, work-group, class. Humanity itself appears ever more as a formless mass to be purposefully "organized."

This is of course conditioned by the population, which, compared to that of earlier ages, has increased disproportionately. The increase has been brought about by science and technology: natural catastrophes are more readily diverted; epidemics are quickly stamped out; hygiene, labor organizations and social welfare agencies create better living and working conditions. However, the increase in population seems to be directly related to a decrease in man's originality. As population mounts, people grow more uniform, and families with genuine tradition and distinction become rarer, the possibilities of leading an individual life get fewer all the time. Modern cities everywhere are alike, whether in Western Europe, China, North or South America, or Russia. A type of man is evolving who lives only in the present, who is "replaceable" to a terrifying degree, and who all too easily falls victim to power.

The modern state shares the characteristics just described. It too is losing its organic structure, becoming more and more a complex of all-controlling functions. In it the human being steps back, the apparatus forward. Constantly improved techniques of stock-taking, man-power survey, and bureaucratic management — to put it brutally, increasingly effective social engineering — tend to treat people much as the machine treats the raw materials fed into it. From the standpoint of the bureaucracy in charge, any resistance on the part of those mistreated is equivalent to revolt, which must be crushed with ever more refined techniques and greater stringency.

As for the peoples of the world, for the time being they continue to be those vast bodies of human beings determined by geography, race and culture who are becoming capable of history within a national framework. Formerly these ethnic groups showed unmistakable individuality, but today they are growing more and more alike. Their mutual economic and political dependence grows constantly greater, their dress and way of life more similar. The nations' political structure and methods of operation are largely interchangeable. This equalizing of ethnic and political individualities seems to contradict the phenomenon of modern nationalism, which has developed in sharp contrast to the unity of the medieval West. The unity, however, was built by spirit and faith, and it left the lives and cultures of the various races their freedom, whereas the levelling process of the modern age springs from the rationality of science and functionalism of technology. Perhaps modern nationalism is the peoples' last attempt to defend themselves against absorption — a defense by means of a formal system which will, however, gradually succumb to other still more abstract principles of power.

When we examine the development as a whole, we cannot escape the impression that nature as well as man himself is becoming ever more vulnerable to the domination — economic, technical, political, organizational — of power. Ever more distinctly our condition reveals itself as one in which man progressively controls nature, yes, but also men; the state controls the citizens; and an autonomous technical-economic-political system holds life in thrall.

The Crisis of Ethical Norms

This growing defenselessness against the inroads of power is furthered by the fact that ethical norms have lost much of their influence, hence their ability to curb abuses of power is weakened.

Ethical norms are valid by their own inner truth, but they become historically effective by taking root in man's vital instincts, inclinations of the soul, social structures, cultural forms and traditions. The process we have been studying breaks these ancient rootholds. They are replaced — at least temporarily — by formalistic rules and regulations and by the various techniques known as "organization." But organization does not create an ethic.

Thus the importance of ethical norms in men's lives gives way to stress on mere expediency. This is true above all of those norms which protect the person. Just one example: Not very long ago, it was considered a sacrilege to dissect a corpse — not, as self-glorifying modernity insists, because the Middle Ages were backward, but because men still harbored an instinctive reverence for the human body, even when dead. From this we can measure the terrible speed with which one bulwark of reticence after the other has been torn down. For the average sentiment, does anything at all remain that is still untouchable? Are not experiments on living bodies performed constantly? Were the practices in certain "scientifically-minded" concentration camps any different from vivisection? Trace the connecting line which leads from control of human conception to interrupted pregnancy; from artificial insemination to euthanasia; from race-breeding to the destruction of undesirable life. What may one *not* do to people if by "one" we mean the average man we encounter everywhere — in the street; in our newspapers; on the screen; radio and television; in literature and drama; and, most ominous of all, in our statesmen, lawmakers, military and economic leaders?

When man drops the ethical reins, he places himself utterly at the mercy of power. Never could he have sunk as low as he did in Germany's all-too-recent past, never could he suffer such abuse as he continues to suffer right now in other parts of the world, had he not been so abandoned by his ethical sense and his feeling for his own personal being. As we have pointed out more than once, a one-sided causality simply does not exist among living beings. One being affects another as much as that other allows himself to be affected, indeed, cooperates in the process. In the long run, domination requires not only the passive consent, but also the will to be dominated, a will eager to drop personal responsibility and personal effort. Broadly speaking, the dominated get what they themselves desire; the inner barriers of self-respect and self-defense must fall before power can really violate.

A further point: life's religious content is steadily disintegrating. This does not necessarily mean that Christian faith is losing its influence on general conditions (though naturally this too can be true), but means something more elemental for man, namely, that the direct religious valuableness of existence is escaping him.

In primitive cultures, everything is religiously determined. Everything significant in man's life and work has a religious root which warrants its existence. The measurements with which he measures; the media he uses for exchange; tool and weapon, threshold and field-marker; the location of the city and its form, determined by the market-place at its heart and the walls which enclose it; natural objects, each with its special significance for man; the animals he hunts — all come from the divine and possess mysterious powers. As critical thought takes over, as man becomes lord of nature, as various natural spheres are abstracted from the original whole, man's awareness of these powers declines.

Modern man cuts himself off not only from the community and from tradition, but also from his religious connections. He is indifferent both to the specific, once-authoritative Christian Credo and to religious ideas in general. Things, forces, processes have become "worldly" — the word stripped of its former religious richness and given a new sense which implies "rationally understandable and technically controllable." This means that man as a whole as well as important individual aspects of human life — the defenselessness of childhood, the special nature of woman, the simultaneous physical weakness and rich experience of the aged — all lose their metaphysical worth. Birth is now considered merely the appearance of a new unit of the species homo sapiens; marriage but an alliance of a man and a woman with certain personal and legal consequences; death the end of a total process known as life. Happiness or unhappiness are no longer providential, but simply lucky or unlucky accidents with which a man must cope as best he can. Things lose their mystery and transparency, becoming calculable forms with specific economic, hygienic and aesthetic values. History no longer bears any relation to a Providence emanating wisdom and benevolence; it is a mere string of empirical processes. The majesty of the state no longer reflects divine majesty; it exists not "by the grace of God," but solely by grace of the people. Or, to put it less irreverently and more sensibly, the state is the organizational apparatus of the people and operates according to psychological, sociological laws. It becomes progressively independent of the people, whom it ultimately dominates completely. All this strengthens and seals the process we described: man, with all he is and has, places himself ever more unreservedly at the disposal of power.

This process leads straight to a concept whose consequences cannot be overestimated: the idea of universal planning. Under such planning man would control everything before him — not only raw materials and natural energies, but also living man in his entirety. Statistics would make an exact inventory of the material at hand; theory would demonstrate the means of utilizing it. "National interest" would determine the general goal; technology would provide the methods with which to attain it.

Universal planning is being prepared with weighty arguments: political necessity, increased population, limited resources and the need for better distribution, the magnitude of modern technical problems, and so forth. But the real drives behind it are spiritual rather than practical. They culminate in an attitude which feels it to be its right and duty to impose its own goal upon mankind, and to utilize all that is as material for the realization of its earthly "kingdom."

Power and Responsibility, pages 38–52 (1951)

The New Culture: Danger

The coming order by which the individual will be related to his or her own works differs radically from the older one. It lacks the precise elements which constituted a culture in the older sense: the feeling of tranquil fertility, of a flowering, beneficent realm. The new culture will be incomparably more harsh and more intense. It will lack the organic both in its sense of growth and of proportions; for the new culture will have been willed into being by the spirit of the human being, built up abstractly by people's own hands. The new culture does not promise that breath necessary for a secure life and free growth; on the contrary, it presents a vision of factories and barracks to the eyes of the mind.

A single fact, we must emphasize, will stamp the new culture: danger. Previously the simplest need for, and the meaning of, culture has always been that culture created security. The experience of the earliest ages teaches us that when people can only see themselves as surrounded by nature, they neither understand themselves nor have they come to terms with their environment. At the dawn of civilization, the order of culture held back the encroaching power of nature, thus making possible an individual's very life. As time moved on, people gained a measure of security. Nature lost its alien or dangerous character and became a spring of inexhaustible plenitude and never-failing rejuvenation. This primitive source of perfection was what the modern person found in nature. Today the situation is being reversed. The course of history has again led us into danger, but the danger confronting us today arises from within culture itself. From the efforts men and women expended and from the fortresses they built to conquer that ancient danger, they created new dangers.

This pervasive threat does not originate in any of the particular difficulties facing people today, nor does it allow that science and technology can yet cope with it. The new danger arises from a factor intrinsic to the work of the individual, even to the work of an individual's spirit. The new danger arises from the factor of power.

To exercise power means, to a degree at least, that one has mastered the given. Power over the given means that a person has succeeded in checking those existential forces which oppose his or her life, that people have bent them to their will. Today the scepter of power is wielded by the hands of men and women. They have extensively mastered the immediate forces of nature, but they have not mastered the mediate forces because they have not yet brought under control their own native powers. People today hold power over things, but we can assert confidently that they do not yet have power over their own power.

Human beings are free; they can use their power as they please. Within their very freedom reside the possibilities of misuse, a misuse which is one with destruction and with evil. What can guarantee an individual's proper use of his or her power in the realm of freedom? Nothing. There is no guarantee that men or women will use their freedom for the good; at best we could have the mere probability that they would use it for the good. We have mentioned already that even a prejudiced observer must conclude that people today lack that rectified character which would ensure their right use of power. As yet they have not developed thoughtfully that ethic which would be effective for controlling the use of power. Moreover, no proper training ground now exists for such an ethic, either with the elite or with the great body of people.

And so it is that the dangers facing human freedom mount ominously day by day. Science and technology have so mastered the forces of nature that destruction, either chronic or acute, and incalculable in extent, is now a possibility. Without exaggeration one can say that a new era of history has been born. Now and forever people will live at the brink of an ever-growing danger which shall leave its mark upon their entire existence.

The End of the Modern World, pages 108–110 (1950)

The New Life: Cosmic Interdependence

Distance and Intimacy

The feeling that is beginning to permeate our own age is that the world is something shaped, hence limited. The measure of those limits is colossal in both directions, great and small, but they *are* measured. The term "all" seems to be acquiring a new significance. No longer does it mean simply the reverence-demanding exaltedness of being as such, nor yet the sum-total of "the given," which not only permits man to take a stand to judge the world, to plan for it, but also demands these things of him. Today it is much easier for man to experience himself as he really is: someone in the world yet "outside" it; bound by its laws yet free to confront it; someone, so to speak, on the edge of the world, everywhere and forever on its frontiers.

This basic feeling begets a different attitude to the world. It is harsher, harder, yet it keeps man's head and hands peculiarly free. The world no longer overpowers; it challenges — a challenge that calls for intellectual-spiritual responsibility.

Something similar is beginning to reveal itself in that field of practical activity which is forced to reckon with the most important of earthly norms, the political — "politics" understood in its real meaning of activities of peoples and governments taken in definite areas at definite times. Modernity could bask in dreams of yet undiscovered lands, untapped reserves. The concept of "colony" was an expression of this. Even the individual peoples and their states embraced, both materially and humanly speaking, unknown, unmeasured possibilities. Hence there was a certain justification for the lighthearted assumption that more substance existed than would be used, more energy than that recorded. Today the world has shrunk to a single political field with no gaps or empty spaces. On the international scene, what were once political objects are becoming, as we watch, political subjects: the phenomenon of the colony is vanishing like smoke. On the national, by means of statistical techniques and intensive administration, the living standards, goods and energies of lands and peoples are known and controlled ever more completely.

As a result, political problems turn more and more from the extensive to the intensive. "Governing" — in the true sense of observing, judging, comprehending, directing, evaluating the given part in view of the whole — becomes particularly urgent. In this closed field every measure has a much sharper effect, for good or for evil. Its force is not dissipated in limitless surroundings, but rings out in closed space, a clear summons to responsibility which cannot pass unheard. Perhaps the pathological growth of bureaucracy presents not only a negative symptom of our times, but also a kernel of truth: historical-political conditions are far more malleable now than formerly, and hence must be approached with greater awareness and precision than in the past. All the bumbling intricacy and crude attempts at leading people around displayed by modern bureaucracy may be reflections of the contemporary state's insufficient comprehension of this fact.

The growing, universal awareness of the world as a unit seems to be another pointer in the same direction. Instead of the earlier atomistic interpretation, according to which existence consisted basically of discrete entities grouped according to viewpoint, we have today an ever deeper realization that all existence rests on certain basic forms, and that the individual form is part of a whole, which in turn is affected by the individual. From this springs the awareness that everything affects everything. Those who remember with what dogmatic certainty end-of-the-century rationalism explained all events by a one-sided causality, dismissing the concept of a final cause as Scholastic humbug, are now amazed at the reappearance of that concept as something "new," and amused to see it applied so radically that we can speak of a reversal of causality, in other words, of a causation working backwards into the past.

Politically, in the broadest meaning of the word, we are approaching a state in which the economic, social, national conditions of one country have repercussions all over the world. Just as no one class in a country can long remain in poor social, economic, or hygienic conditions without affecting the whole nation, so also no particular group can flourish long and truly when conditions as a whole are not in good order.

Indeed, people are beginning to realize that the same sort of interdependence that exists between individuals and groups also holds true for religious and secular attitudes. In our own time we have seen modernity's insistence on the private nature of a man's *Weltanschauung* [worldview] completely overturned. The dogmatic, all-encompassing control so popularly ascribed to the Middle Ages was sheer liberalism compared with that exercised by National Socialism and progressively developed and perfected by Communism. Let us for a moment disregard the violation of all truths and human dignity that was and is largely practiced by such systems — it is significant that they found they could not leave any aspect of existence out of account. What we call personal freedom, independence, self-possession must be quite different from what the old liberal attitude thought them to be; rather, the inner world in which a man lives with himself is intimately linked with the reality of existence. The view that religion is something purely subjective, and the opposite view that it is to be determined by the state are so closely related that they may be regarded as two facets of the same fundamental error.

In the realm of immediate fundamental values, present-day biology and medicine realize with growing clarity that the function of the individual organ affects the whole organism, and conversely, the condition of the whole is shared by each part. Hence there is no physical ailment that is not psychologically conditioned, just as every psychic-intellectual process presupposes specific physical conditions.

The broadest expression of this tendency in current thought may be found in the growing importance of the concept of relativity. By this I do not mean the disintegrating relativism of the foregoing epoch, which stripped given conditions of their own special worth, constantly referring each aspect back to the preceding one and so destroying the original phenomenon. If I understand it correctly, today's conception of relativity gives it a new and different significance. It attempts to show that being is always a totality, the various aspects of which exist with, through, and in relation to one another. This is seen in such elementary phenomena as the act of knowing, in which the object cannot be considered apart from the subject, in which the observer and the observed coinhere; or again, in regard to causality, in which there exist no one-sided effects among beings, but every effect is bipolar.

Thus here too we have the phenomenon of comprehensiveness in good as in evil. Hence, what should be demanded of any proper governance or "rule" is that it be firmly grounded in knowledge of how the various energies of existence affect one another, and in a deep sense of responsibility for existence, whose many reciprocal effects render it especially vulnerable.

Tradition and Novelty

The modern world view conceived of a nature that was as much its own norm as it was a system of security. Nature was considered to be a complicated apparatus of laws and interrelations which on the one hand bound man, and on the other safeguarded and warranted his existence. Today, knowledge and technology are breaking up the natural forms. Even the elements are open to seizure. Once a sovereign and protective harmony, nature today is a mere sum of matter and energies under man's control. Once an inviolable, awe- and joy-inspiring whole, nature is becoming an inexhaustible Possibility, Dynamo, Workshop. And whereas in the modern age man considered himself a part or "member" of nature, the feeling today is that he can "handle" it in unlimited freedom, bending it to his will for prosperity or destruction.

Similar changes are affecting also the inherited patterns of existence and the various forms of tradition, which in the West were stamped by Christianity and Humanism, and in Asia and Africa by their own religious-cultural past. Once the individual participated fully in his tradition; he was both shaped and protected by it. Today tradition everywhere is disintegrating. Characteristically, novelty is now accepted as value *per se*. The desire to change everything seems to be more than a mere symptom of change in generations, more than the discoverer's eagerness to prove the importance of his discovery. Naturally enough, it has negative forms: irreverence, irresponsibility, sensationalism. But beneath these something positive seems at work: the feeling that to a degree hitherto undreamed, the world lies at man's disposal; and that man's right use of the world is guaranteed neither by nature nor by tradition, but depends upon his personal insight and will.

We have already discussed at some length the element of danger that lies herein, so we need only remind ourselves of it once more. It does not belong exclusively to the negative symptoms of the coming culture. If it did, we could only conclude: then away with it! But danger is an integral part of the coming world view, and when rightly understood, it lends that view a new earnestness. To the end of time there will be no human existence that does not live with peril.

Awareness of this is lively, and not without the usual unworthy companions of fear, superficiality, the eat-drink-and-be-merry-now attitude we meet everywhere. But it has its positive symptoms too; the bourgeois devotion to security seems to be waning, and man is beginning to free himself from many involvements that formerly he took for granted. The fact that entire populations have been uprooted and transplanted, that the old conception of home is fast disappearing and an almost nomadic form of life is taking its place, that people today have lost interest in savings accounts and are changing their attitude to the various types of insurance — all this and more suggests not only the negative aspect of general rootlessness, but also a positive: that in response to the unknown, unknowable dangers of the future, man is attempting to gain a larger measure of mobility. The feeling is growing that everything is an open question, because ultimately everything depends on freedom; therefore man himself must develop an attitude of greater freedom. What a curious development this is, hard on the heels of classical natural science, according to which everything was determined by necessity and hence was insurable!

Lastly, characteristic of the nascent world are its markedly greater mobility, flexibility, potentialities, as compared with those of the world view which preceded it.

Power and Responsibility, pages 67–74 (1951)

Building the Emerging World

What, then, ought he to look like, the new human architect of that emerging world?

He must know and agree that the import of the coming culture is not welfare but dominion, fulfillment of man's God-given assignment to rule over the earth. What is needed is not universal insurance, but the kind of world in which human sovereignty with its greatness can express itself. This is not what the average citizen desired. He feared it, indeed, felt it to be a fundamentally wrong ideal. That is why he exercised the power he did possess with an uneasy conscience, feeling it necessary to justify it with "security," "utility," "welfare." That is why his governing is without a true ethos, why it has created no genuine government architecture, style, or tradition — because it has taken refuge in anonymity. The man we envision must unhesitatingly place security, utility, and welfare second; the greatness of the coming world image must be placed first.

With this we come to the second basic need: an elemental relationship to technology. The creators of technology failed to assimilate their own creation into their sense of life. When a nineteenth-century industrialist built himself a house, the result was either a palace or a castle. The generation born between the World Wars feels differently. Here is a type of human being who lives in harmony with technology. With an ease that astounds nontechnical minds, he moves among the technical patterns of his day. Thus he possesses the freedom that is necessary if man is to prevail.

The new man we have in mind is also profoundly aware of the dangers inherent in present-day conditions. Since Hiroshima we know that we live on the rim of disaster, and that we shall stay there till the end of history. The new type of man senses the danger; he fears it, too, naturally, but he does not succumb to that fear, for it is familiar to him. He has grown up with it. He recognizes and faces it. In fact, it forms the kernel of a certain exhilarating sense of greatness. Current (in its extreme form "beatnik") contempt for bourgeois dependence on carefully precalculated security; the revolutionary change in man's relation to home and property; certain tendencies in modern art, philosophy and so forth — all seem to point that way. The man in question can live with danger, or at least knows that he can and must learn to. Yet he does not treat danger as a mere adventure; his typical reaction to it is a sense of responsibility for the world.

The New Freedom

[The new man] has overcome the modern dogma: all things of themselves are for the best. For him the optimism of the progress-worshipper no longer exists. He knows from experience that left to themselves, things just as readily retrogress. He knows that the world is in the hands of freedom; hence, he feels responsibility for tomorrow's kind of freedom. And love, his love of the world is very special, deepened by the precariousness, vulnerability and helplessness of his beloved. To his respect for power and greatness, his comfortable relationships to technology and his will to utilize it, to the zest of looking danger in the eye, he adds another quality, chivalry, not to say tenderness, toward finite, oh-so-jeopardized existence.

A further trait is his acceptance of absolute demands. The coming man is definitely un-liberal, which does not mean that he has no respect for freedom. The "liberal" attitude is that which declines to incorporate absolutes into existence because their either-or engenders struggle. It is far easier to be able to see things in any light, "the only important thing" being "life" and "getting along with others." Values and ideas are but a matter of personal opinion. Leave everybody alone, and all will be well. The man under discussion knows that unfreed from such attitudes man can never cope with the existential situation we face today. What will count will be not details or elaborations, but fundamentals; dignity or slavery; growth or decline; truth or lie; the mind or the passions.

This man knows how to command as well as how to obey. He respects discipline not as a passive, blind "being integrated into" a system, but as the responsible discipline which stems from his own conscience and personal honor. Here is the prerequisite for the greatest task he faces — the task of establishing an authority which respects human dignity and of creating a social order in which the person can exist. The ability to command and to obey has been lost in the degree that faith and doctrine have disappeared from man's consciousness. As a result, in the place of unconditional truth, we have catchwords: instead of command, compulsion; instead of obedience, self-abandonment. What real command and real obedience are must be rediscovered. This is possible only when absolute sovereignty is recognized and absolute values are accepted — in other words, when God is acknowledged as the living norm and point of reference for all existence. Ultimately, one can command only from God, obey only in him.

The new man also appreciates asceticism again. He knows that there is no authority which does not begin with the command of self, that no orderly form of existence can be established by anyone who is not, himself, "formed." There is no greatness which is not grounded deep in self-conquest and self-denial. Man's instincts are not of themselves orderly; they must be put (and kept) in order. Man must master them, not they him. Faith in the so-called goodness of nature is cowardice. It is a refusal to face the evil that is there too, along with the good. Thus the good loses its depth and earnestness. The evil in nature must be resisted, and this resistance is asceticism. Real, unqualified command, which stems not from force but from valid authority; real, unqualified obedience, which is not self-abandonment but recognition of legitimate competence — these are possible only when man overcomes the direct impact of his instincts and inclinations. The man to come will have to rediscover that liberating power lies in self-control; that inwardly accepted suffering transforms the sufferer; and that all existential growth depends not on effort alone, but also on freely offered sacrifice.

Relevant to this is something we have glimpsed at various points — namely, companionship between man and man. This is not the respectless familiarity of barracks and camp nor the tired remnants of that ethos which insists that life's challenges are meaningless and that all grounds of confidence, greatness, and joy have crumbled away. It is the natural solidarity of those who stand shoulder to shoulder at the common task, in common danger; it is the self-understood readiness for mutual help and for the integration of individual efforts. It also possesses that unqualified character often engendered by and transcending the particular bonds of blood and sympathy.

From what has been said it must be clear that what is needed is not a new version of Sparta. The new type man is as apt to be a soldier as he is to be a priest, a businessman as a farmer, a doctor as an artist, a factory worker as a research scientist. He certainly must not be appraised by his toughness alone. All too many in Germany fell victim not so long ago to the "heroic" ideals of "fanatic will," "dogged determination," "ruthless sacrifice"! Those who tossed those slogans about so freely were in reality not strong but weak: they were violent from personal uncertainty, brutal from paucity of heart. And if they actually were fearless in the face of danger, it was because for them the spirit counted as nothing. The strength we mean comes straight from the spirit, from the heart's voluntary surrender; that is why it nurtures all that is known as reverence, magnanimity, goodness, considerateness, interiority.

Religion

One final trait in this image of man: his religious attitude.

Should the possibility of a world dominion such as we have tried to suggest be felt generally, an objective, this-worldly will to work and to govern might come into existence which would reject everything metaphysical as obstructive. But, even then, the tremendousness of the task ahead would force people to take reality seriously, and this in turn would lead to the realization that the world can be mastered only along the lines of truth, whole truth, hence in obedience to the essence of things.

Precisely here, in such obedience, lies the seed of a very real piety. The mind which considers reality not from any subjective *a priori,* but purely objectively, is more inclined than the subjective, unscientific, undisciplined mind to discover that finiteness is also createdness. It has been prepared to grasp the revealed nature of everything that is, and from there to reach a decisive affirmation of Biblical Revelation. By this process a completely unsentimental, in the purest sense of the word, *realistic* piety would evolve, a piety no longer operating in a separate realm of psychological interiority or religious idealism, but within reality, a reality which, because complete, is also the reality created, sustained and willed by God.

From the depth of clarity such as this the new man would also be able to see through the illusions which reign in the midst of scientific and technological development: the deception behind the "liberal's" idolatry of culture; behind the totalitarian's utopia, the tragicist's pessimism; behind modern mythicism and the hermaphrodite world of psychoanalysis. He would see and know for himself: Reality is simply not like that! These paths lead away from [reality], not to it. Man is not so constructed, and neither is life. We may place high hope in the power of direct insight which belongs to this new realism.

Moreover, the objective mind seems to run a good chance of grasping Christianity's innermost secret: humility; to appreciate its transforming power (truly an intellectual-spiritual splitting of the existential atom); and to make it the extricating energy for life's seemingly inextricable tangle. From all this could come something like true dominion.

Power and Responsibility, pages 83–90 (1951)

Possibilities of Action

Nature and Spirit

Modern man, whom we have discussed at some length, likes to consider history as the unreeling of a necessary process. This view is an after-effect of the modern concept of nature as the basic data of that which is. If this is true, then it must follow that all that takes place in nature is natural, hence right. Now actually, history is determined by the spirit, but according to the above theory, even the spirit is a mere part of that universal whole whose "rightness" finds expression within the framework of nature. Therefore, all the mistakes, abuses, violence of individuals in history are scrupulously ignored: the process of history is a "natural" process, hence right and trustworthy.

One of the main decisions which future man will have to make will turn on his realizing or failing to realize the error of this concept. Man is determined by the spirit, but the spirit is *not* "nature." The spirit lives and acts neither by historical nor by metaphysical necessity, but of its own impulse. It is free. It draws its ultimate life and health from its right relation to the true and the good, a relation which it is also free to deny or destroy. Man does not belong exclusively to the world; rather he stands on its borders, at once in the world yet outside it, integrated into it yet simultaneously dealing with it because he is related directly to God. Not to the "Spirit of the Age," not to the "All-Mysterious One," not to any First Cause — but to the sovereign Lord, Creator of all being, who called man into existence and sustains him in that vocation, who gave the world into his keeping, and who will demand an account of what he has done with it.

Thus history does not run on its own; it is run. It can also be run badly. And not only in view of certain decisions or for certain stretches of the road and in certain areas; its whole direction can be off course for whole epochs, centuries long. This we know or at least suspect, for all our confidence in our experimental and theoretical precision. It is this "suspicion" which gives our situation its special poignancy.

Man is being given ever more power of decision and control over world reality, but man himself is removing himself further and further from the norms which spring from the truth of being and from the demands of goodness and holiness. Thus his decisions are in danger of becoming increasingly fortuitous.

For this reason the basic answer to the question "What can be done?" must run something like this: First of all, man must accept the full measure of his responsibility; but also to be able to do this he must regain his right relation to the truth of things, to the demands of his own deepest self, and finally to God. Otherwise he becomes the victim of his own power, and the forecast of "global catastrophe" quoted earlier will really become inevitable.

When we said that the spirit is not determined by natural necessity but must act in freedom, we did not mean that man himself must establish the meaning of events. It is worth noting that both extreme existentialism and the totalitarian state believe that he must, thus proclaiming themselves opposite poles of the same basic will: to use power arbitrarily, which means to misuse it as violence. In reality, everything that exists is shaped in a meaningful form which provides acting man with the norm from which to draw the possible and the right. Freedom does not consist in following our personal or political predilections, but in doing what is required by the essence of things.

All this means first of all that we must know where the historical changes discussed above are leading; we must ascertain their underlying causes and face the problems they involve. This is the task to which schools and universities must apply themselves if they are not to fall by the wayside of time. Important too are those forms of research and effort which have developed along with the pedagogical labors of the last fifty years and which have consolidated in vocational workshops, holiday conferences, academies and various special institutes. The sociological "place" of such attempts at better understanding lies between school and university, between the individual question and consolidated research efforts of the profession. Thus they are well suited for the task of tracing forces in the making, and responsible authorities have good reason to encourage them. Not to influence them — for that would only destroy the opportunities peculiar to free experiment — but to allow for them, to support them and to cooperate with them in a form which remains to be found.

The modern age was inclined to grapple with necessary innovations by means of rational intellect and organization. The problems which face us today are so gigantic that we must reach for a deeper hold.

Now that science has begun to break up the natural elements, something analogous must take place on the human level: man must examine the basic facts of his existence. If he does not, events will pass him by, leaving him an ever greater stranger on earth. In the main, men agree that technology, economics, politics must be directed "realistically," but what they mean is in a manner which totally disregards ultimate values: man's personal destiny and all that is God's due. This lopsided attitude is just as unrealistic and out-of-date as that which regards the phenomenon of illness only physically, ignoring its psychological-biological aspects. Medicine is coming to realize ever more clearly to what extent the soul determines the body's health or illness, and that only the diagnosis which encompasses the patient's whole reality, including his spiritual-intellectual life, can really claim to be realistic. The same is true here. Already not a few people listen with neither derision nor skepticism when the pains of our age are diagnosed clearly: what the sick would need is a *metanoia,* a conversion, a reappraisal of our whole attitude toward life, accompanied by a fundamental change in the climate in which people and things are appraised. It is to them, those in search of a genuine realism, that the following is addressed.

Let us be explicit. Have we ever stopped to consider exactly what takes place when the average superior assigns a task to a subordinate . . . when the average school teacher teaches a class or maintains discipline . . . judge decides a case . . . priest champions the things of God . . . doctor treats a patient . . . bureaucrat deals with the public in his office . . . industrialist directs his firm . . . merchant supplies his customers . . . factory-worker tends his machine . . . farmer runs his farm? Is it really clear to us in each concrete process what the decisive intention and attitude was, and what its direct and indirect results? Was the truth in each case protected, its particular validity trusted? Did the person encountered go away feeling that he had been treated with dignity, that he had been received as a person by a person? Did that other appeal to his freedom, to all that is vital and creative in him? Together did they reach the heart of the matter, broaching it as it was meant to be broached, essentially?

The objection that these are private matters of no historical importance does not hold. Every historical process, even the most dynamic, is made up of just such situations, and the way they are dealt with is what gives each phase in history its particular mold. It is exactly here that the shoe we are wearing pinches: these elementary things, which we ought to be able to take for granted, we no longer can take for granted. Of course, in earlier epochs also truth, justice, personal dignity and contact with others' central creativity were not always, possibly not even generally, protected; but they certainly were acknowledged and at least in theory taken seriously. The tendency to respect them was there, and the man of good will could easily, at any time, step from the general acknowledgement of their importance to his own particular realization of them. This has changed, to our culture's growing uneasiness. The lack of human warmth and dignity in our contacts with "the world" is what chills the heart, and what lurks at the bottom of the growing feeling that things are no longer "right." The fact must be recognized and accepted that even the most commonplace "public relations" are *not* a matter of private morality, but the life blood of every historical process and public policy, and that on them will depend the health or death of our political and cultural existence.

Let us attempt the difficult and thankless task of suggesting a few practical points of view.

Essential to any really practical suggestion is its workability, so let us try to get down to brass tacks, even at the risk of sounding "moralistic." Actually, many people, the most dispassionate and unbiased realists, continue to live according to much-abused "morality," and it is they, not the "free spirits," who uphold existence.

Contemplation

First, we must try to rediscover something of what is called the contemplative attitude, actually experiencing it ourselves, not just talking about it interestingly. All around us we see activity, organization, operations of every possible type; but what directs them? An inwardness no longer really at home within itself which thinks, judges, acts from the surface, guided by mere intellect, utility, and the impulses of power, property and pleasure. An "interiority" too superficial to contact the truth lying at life's center, which no longer reaches the essential and everlasting, but remains somewhere just under the skin-level of the provisional and the fortuitous.

Before all else, then, man's depths must be reawakened. His life must again include times, his day moments of stillness in which he collects himself and spreads out before his heart the problems which have stirred him during the day. In a word, man must learn again to meditate and to pray. How, we cannot say. This depends largely on his basic beliefs, his religious position, his temperament and surroundings. But in any case, he must step aside from the general hustle and bustle; he must become tranquil and really "there," opening his mind and heart wide to some word of piety or wisdom or ethical honor, whether he takes from Scripture or Plato, from Goethe or Jeremias Gotthelf. He must accept the criticism which that particular word suggests to him, examining some related aspect of his own life in its beam. Only an attitude this deeply grounded in truth can gain a stand against the forces around us.

Next, we must pose the elementary question as to the essence of things.

One look is enough to reveal how schematic is our attitude to things; what slaves of convention we are; how superficially — from the criteria of mere advantage, ease and time-savings — we approach things. Yet each thing has an essence. When this is ignored or abused, a resistance is built up which neither cunning nor violence can overcome. Then reality bolts its doors against man's grasp. The order of things is destroyed. The axles of the economic, social, political wagons run hot. No, man cannot use things as he pleases, at least not generally, and not for long. He can use them only essentially, as they were meant to be used, with impunity. Otherwise he invites catastrophe. Anyone who uses his eyes can see the catastrophic results of mishandled reality.

Therefore we must return to the essence of being and ask: What is the connection between a man's work and his life? What must justice and law be like if they are to further rather than hinder? What is property, its rights, its abuses? What is genuine command and what makes it possible? What is obedience, and how is it related to freedom? What do health, sickness, death really signify? What friendship, comradeship? When may attraction claim the high name of love? What does the union of man and woman known as marriage mean (at present something so seedy, so choked with weed, that few people seem to have any serious conception of it, although it is the bearer of all human existence)? Does such a thing as a scale of values exist? Which of its values is the most important, which the least?

These are the elemental realities we live from, for, with. We deal with them constantly, arrange and reshape them — but do we know what they are? Apparently not, or we would not treat them so casually. So we had better find out what they are, and not merely with a detached rationality, but by penetrating them so deeply that we are shaken by their power and significance.

Command of Self

Further, we must learn again that command over the world presupposes command of self. For how can men control the growing monstrousness of power when they cannot even control their own appetites? How can they shape political or cultural decisions affecting countless others, when they are continually failing themselves?

There was a time when philosophers, historians and poets used the word "asceticism" as an expression of "medieval hostility to life," and advocated instead a life lived in search of "experience," of immediate sensation. Today much of this has changed, at least with those whose thinking and judging stem from responsibility. At any rate, we do well to realize at last that there has never been greatness without asceticism, and what is needed today is something not only great, but ultimate: we must decide whether we are going to realize the requirements of rule in freedom or slavery.

An ascetic is a man who has himself well in hand. To be capable of this, he must recognize the wrongs within himself and set about righting them. He must regulate his physical as well as his intellectual appetites and educate himself to hold his possessions in freedom, sacrificing the lesser for the greater. He must fight for inner health and freedom — against the machinations of advertising, the flood of loud sensationalism, against noise in all its forms. He must acquire a certain distance from things; he must train himself to think independently, to resist what "they" say. Street, traffic, newspaper, radio, screen and television all present problems of self-discipline, indeed of the most elementary self-defense — problems we hardly suspect, to say nothing of tackling. Everywhere man is capitulating to the forces of barbarism. Asceticism is the refusal to capitulate, the determination to fight them at the key bastion — namely ourselves. It means that through self-discipline and self-restraint man develops from the core outward, holding life high in honor so that it may be fruitful on the level of its deepest significance.

Further, we must weigh again, in all earnestness, the existential question of our ultimate relation to God.

Man is not constructed to be complete in himself and, in addition, capable of entering into relations with God or not as he sees fit. His very essence consists in his relation to God and what he understands by that relationship; how seriously he takes it and what he does about it are the determining factors of his character. This is so, and no philosopher, politician, poet or psychologist can change it.

It is dangerous to ignore realities, for they have a way of avenging themselves. When instincts are suppressed or conflicts kept alive, neuroses set in. God is the Reality on whom all other realities, including the human, are founded. When existence fails to give him his due, existence sickens.

Finally: Do everything that is to be done with respect for the truth; do it in freedom of spirit, in spite of the obstacles within and without, and in the teeth of selfishness, sloth, cowardice, popular opinion. And do it with confidence.

By this I do not mean to follow a program of any kind, but to make the simple responses that always were and always will be right: not to wait until someone in need asks for help, but to offer it; to perform every official act in a manner befitting both common sense and human dignity; to declare the truth when its "hour" has come, even when it will bring down opposition or ridicule; to accept responsibility when the conscience considers it a duty.

When one so acts, he paves the road which, followed with sincerity and courage, leads far — no one can say how far — into the realm where the great things of Time are decided.

It may seem strange that our consideration of universal problems should end on the most personal level possible. But as the subtitle of this book indicates, it is an attempt to set a course. What would be the sense of developing ideas while ignoring the point from which they can be realized or fail to be realized? It cannot have escaped the reader that in these pages we have not tried to present programs or panaceas, but to free the initiative for fruitful action.

Power and Responsibility, pages 92–104 (1951)

The Task

The old world is perishing — "world" in the broadest sense of the term, the epitome of works and institutions and orders and living attitudes. The middle of the nineteenth century was the historical turning point. (Naturally the roots go back much further.) To that world belonged a certain view of humanity that was common despite all the many and great differences. That world was sustained by human beings and in turn sustained them. Human beings created it and gave it life. They kept it alive and in their hands. It was their work, expression, object and instrument, all at the same time. That was culture, and what we still have in the way of culture derives from it.

But then came new events of a different type, proportion and starting point, and with a different goal. The forces on which they rested were different and so was their relation to nature.

With these new events, the old order collapsed, and those who supported it, whose blood to some extent we all carry, were homeless. Indeed, they dissolved inwardly, for the older world existed through them and they through it. The new events did not just break into the objective order as a matter of objective culture. They also, and above all, broke into our living humanity. The development of technology is primarily an inner human process; hence, we are homeless in the midst of barbarism. This is true when we look at things from the point of view of the past, for that is to feel our environment collapsing, and ourselves with it. It is also true when we look at things from the standpoint of what is new both without and within, for then all is still chaos.

. . . Into the ancient picture of humanity and the world has burst a new and very different type of being and event. This new thing is destructive because it affects those who do not belong to it. More precisely, it is chaotic and destructive because those who do belong to it are not yet on the scene. It is destructive because it is not under human control. It is a surging ahead of unleashed forces that have not yet been mastered, raw material that has not yet been put together, giving a living and spiritual form related to humanity. Mastering such raw materials and forces — collecting, shaping, and relating them, and thus creating a world of culture — is something that those who are oriented to the old world cannot do. They do not have the norms or concepts or power for the task. On the older plane the battle for living culture has been lost, and we feel the profound helplessness of those who are old. The battle must now be joined on a new plane. Totally technical events and unleashed forces can be mastered only by a new human attitude that is a match for them. We must put mind, spirit and freedom to work afresh. But we must relate this new effort to the new events, the new matter and style and inner orientations. It must have its living starting point, its fulcrum, where the process itself begins.

Are the processes only variations on a common theme, or is something historically new irrupting in them? If it is — and I am convinced this is so — then we must say yes to it. I know what this yes costs. Those who are already naively saying it, and those who are able to make rapid switches, will see in the deliberations of these letters only a romantic looking back, a tie to what is past. This may give them a feeling of complacency. Yet there is a yes to what is happening historically that is a decision because it springs from a knowing heart. Such a yes has weight. Our place is in what is evolving. We must take our place, each at the right point. We must not oppose what is new and try to preserve a beautiful world that is inevitably perishing. Nor should we try to build a new world of the creative imagination that will show none of the damage of what is actually evolving. Rather, we must transform what is coming to be. But we can do this only if we honestly say yes to it and yet, with incorruptible hearts, remain aware of all that is destructive and nonhuman in it. Our age has been given to us as the soil on which to stand and the task to master.

At bottom we would not wish it otherwise. Our age is not just an external path that we tread; it is ourselves. Our age is our own blood, our own soul. We relate to it as to ourselves. We love it and hate it at one and the same time. As we are, so we relate to it. If we are thoughtless, we relate to it thoughtlessly. If we say yes to it in the form of a decision, then it is because we have had to come to a decision vis-à-vis ourselves.

We love the tremendous power of the age and its readiness for responsibility. We love the resoluteness with which it hazards itself and pushes things to extremes. Our soul is touched by something great that might well emerge. We love it, and our soul is touched, even though we see clearly its questionability relative to the value of the past age. We must be able to see very plainly what is at issue if with a fixed heart we are ready to sacrifice the inexpressible nobility of the past.

The New Humanity

Nor is it true that what is taking place is not Christian. The minds at work in it may often be non-Christian, but the events as such are not. It is Christianity that has made possible science and technology and all the results from them. Only those who had been influenced by the immediacy of the redeemed soul to God and the dignity of the regenerate, so that they were aware of being different from the world around them, could have broken free from the tie to nature in the way that this has been done in the age of technology. The people of antiquity would have been afraid of hubris here. [Only those to whom the relationship with God gave a sense of the unconditional, only those to whom the parable of the treasure hidden in the field . . . showed that there is something for which everything must be given up, were capable of the kind of decision for something ultimate that is dominant in science today and in its search for truth, even should this make life impossible, or in technology today in its pressing ahead, even should this call all human existence into question with its transformation of the world.] Only those to whom Christian faith had given profound assurance about eternal life had the confidence that such an undertaking requires. But the forces, of course, have broken free from the hands of living personalities. Or should we say that the latter could not hold them and let them go free? These forces have thus fallen victim to the demonism of number, machine and the will for domination.

In appropriate activity we now have to penetrate the new thing so as to gain mastery over it. We have to become lords of the unleashed forces and shape them into a new order that relates to humanity. In the last resort only living people, not the tackling of technological problems themselves, can do this. There are, of course, technological and scientific tasks, but people have to perform them. A new humanity must emerge of more profound intelligence, new freedom, new inwardness, new form, new ability to give form. It must be of such a kind that it already has new events in all the fibers of its being and in its manner of apprehension. The new science may be monstrous, the economic and political organization gigantic, the technology powerful when measured by the standards of living science, economy, politics and technology, but they are only raw material. What we need is not less technology but more. Or, more accurately, we need stronger, more considered, more human technology. We need more science, but it must be more intellectual and designed; we need more economic and political energy, but it must be more mature and responsible, able to see the details in the whole contexts to which it belongs. All of that is possible, however, only if living people first make their influence felt in the sphere of objective nature, if they relate this nature to themselves and in this way create a "world" again.

We have to create a world again out of the most monstrous raw materials and forces of all kinds. We originally confronted the task of having to assert ourselves vis-à-vis nature, which then threatened us on all sides because it had not been mastered by us and was thus a chaos for us. "Fill the earth and subdue it"; that chaos — from our standpoint — was shaped into a human world. To the extent that we did this — taking possession of the world and achieving security over against it and in it — by this creativity we have released new forces that had not yet been released by our own attitude and the form of the world we had created. These forces have increased, and now they have unleashed a new chaos. In the spiral line of history we are now over the point where the first task confronted the race, that of creating a "world." We are again threatened on all sides, this time by chaos that results from our own creating.

Saying Yes

We must first say yes to our age. We cannot solve the problem by retreating or simply seeking to alter or improve it. Only a new initiative can bring a solution. It has to be possible to tread the path of developing awareness until we achieve an inner standard, not one imposed by external limitations. It has to be possible at the same time to attain a new inner security independent of what is burning in that awareness, an attitude of respect that supports the knowledge, a new naiveté of consciousness, an ability to believe in the midst of skepticism. It has to be possible also to dispel illusion, to see the limits of existence sharply drawn, and yet to attain to a new infinitude that proceeds from mind and spirit.

Further, it must be possible to tackle the task of mastering nature in a way that is appropriate, but also to find a new sphere of freedom for the soul; to give back true security to life; to achieve an attitude, a disposition, a new order of living, standards of what is excellent and what is despicable, of what is permissible and what is impermissible, of responsibility, of limits, etc., by which we can hold in check the danger of destruction presented by arbitrary natural forces.

We must be willing to see the older aristocracy of small numbers vanish, to accept the fact of everything in mass, to accept the fact that even among the masses each person has rights and life and goods, yet also to bring integration and to arrive at a new ranking of value and humanity.

Finally, it has to be possible to follow the technological path to a meaningful goal, to let technological forces develop with their own dynamic even though in the process the old order perishes, but out of these powers of an adult humanity to create a new order, a new cosmos.

All of this has to be possible, but is it realistic? Within the older human level on which we stand it is not. That is why we see helplessness on every hand. There is much zealous work, but one detects impotence. The unleashed forces have to be mastered on a new level, from a new standpoint, in terms of a new view of things. Systems and ideas will not produce this, only human beings themselves. The emergence of a new, free, strong and well-formed humanity is needed, one that would be a match for these forces.

Is it not fantasy to hope for anything of this kind? Can we rationally count on the possibility of such a new humanity emerging? Or are we just comforting ourselves with fine words?

. . . What we have here is the emergence of a new and deep stratum of the human. If we were to say to chemists that now that we know the elements and forces all the possibilities of mass and energy are exhausted, they would reply that the most gigantic possibility is still ahead of us. This has now manifested itself, just as tremendous energy is released by splitting the atom. We have here a symbol of what I have in mind. In the inner human world an analogous deep force has to emerge that will give a new freedom from the world and a very profound way of seeing and relating to it. Then the event might well take place that was not possible on the older level. We reach here a new level.

I believe that this will come. I cannot prove this, but it seems to me that it is giving intimation of itself. We cannot, of course, bring this to pass by individual decisions or organizations. It is a comprehensive historical event even though it takes place in the individual person. It is an event whose starting point is not accessible to us.

. . . Most hopeful of all, I constantly see individuals meeting one another with a capacity for true brotherliness — no longer the older organically hierarchical form, but also no longer the organization of the last fifty years with its external dividing and integrating! The new types are convincing and self-evident. They are not like the older liberty and equality; there is a disciplined and intrinsic relating. A dynamic core exists that has within it possibilities of order, ranking, higher and lower, yet also of the anchoring of the one in the loyalty and responsibility of the other.

Moreover, I have a sense of increasing profundity. People today are no longer so sure and arrogant in the sphere of physical and psychological reality as they were in the 1890s. It is as if an inner sphere were opening and drawing us in. A yearning is there for the inward, for quiet, for leaving the mad rush and refocusing. Yet this refocusing will not negate other being and action but will take place within it. We sense possibilities of concentration and inwardness in the everyday, in life as it is. I believe that technology, the economy and politics need such quiet and inner fervor if they are to do their respective jobs.

Our age is so uncertain, skeptical, seeking and homeless that there are not a few today, I believe, who stand directly before God. Those who stand in the world have need of a stance in themselves and in something deeper than themselves from which to come to grips with the world again. And indeed a wave is moving out from God and reaching our innermost limit beyond which is the other. It is possible that people may talk together and act and spin out their destinies without a single mention of God, and yet be full of him. In this context the question that faces us will be decided. Will we come to God from the depths of our being, link ourselves to him, and in his freedom and power master chaos in this coming age? Will there be people who place themselves totally at God's disposal and alone with and before him make the true decisions? I detect all these forces at work — a powerful upsurging, an inner self-opening, an emergence of form on every hand.

Dear friend, what I have written in this letter is weak compared to the question in others. At bottom I do not know what else to say except that from my heart's core I believe that God is at work. History is going forward in the depths, and we must be ready to play our part, trusting in what God is doing and in the forces that he has made to stir within us.

Letters from Lake Como, pages 78–87, 94–96 (1927)

Chapter 2

Our Life — Today and Tomorrow

Anxiety

With the breakdown of the old world picture, men and women came to feel not only that they had been placed in a life of strange contradictions, but also that their very existence was threatened. Modern people awoke to that anxiety which menaces them to this day, an anxiety not found in the medieval world. Medieval people did experience anxieties; that experience is one with human nature. Indeed people have always known anxiety, and even if science and technology succeed in giving them the appearance of security they will continue to know anxiety. But the causes and the nature of anxiety differ with differing times. Medieval anxiety resulted from the tensions experienced by the soul which although set in a limited universe — one controlled strictly in direction and scope of movement — was bent upon leaping into infinity. Yet medieval tensions were resolved as the soul achieved an ever new and greater transcendence. Modern anxiety, by contrast, arises from a person's deep-seated consciousness that he or she lacks either a real or a symbolic place in reality. In spite of their actual position on earth, they are beings without security. The very needs of people's senses are left unsatisfied, since they have ceased to experience a world which guarantees them a place in the total scheme of existence.

The End of the Modern World, page 52 (1950)

Nature

The new picture of reality was dominated by a number of conceptions, the most important of which was the modern view of Nature. It had come to signify whatever was given immediately to the mind and sensibilities of an individual. It was all those things which existed in the world prior to anything people did to them; it was also the sum total of energy, matter, essences and natural laws. Thus Nature was readily made a matter of value in itself. It became the norm which guided a person in action and in reason toward whatever was right or healthful or perfect. The constant norm was simply natural. From this attitude grew a new ethic. The person who was morally good was the natural person; so too was the natural society or form of government or manner of education or way of life. From the sixteenth to the twentieth century we find this pervasive concept in many guises: in the *honnête homme* of the sixteenth and seventeenth centuries, in the "natural man" of Rousseau, in the rationalism of the Enlightenment, in the "natural" beauty invoked by neoclassicism.

Nature, in short, signified and determined something final beyond which it was impossible to venture. Everything derived from the concept of Nature was understood to be an absolute; whatever could be made to conform with Nature was justified by its very conformity. Yet the conception did not allow that Nature could be understood *qua* Nature. On the contrary, Nature contained within itself the mystery of the primitive origin and end of all things. She was Divine, an object for religious worship; she was praised as creative, wise, benevolent; she was Mother Nature to whose truth people surrendered themselves unconditionally. The Natural had become the Holy and the Good.

The End of the Modern World, pages 52–53 (1950)

Destroy or Build?

The modern mind took culture to be a "natural" thing. We know, of course, that culture is not natural in any real sense; indeed, true culture rests upon the ability of the human spirit both to distinguish itself from and to stand opposite to the natural order of things surrounding it. For the modern consciousness, however, nature and spirit were formed into a unified whole, a whole which constituted the totality of being, creation itself, and in which everything was regulated by absolute laws. Nature and spirit formed a world, therefore, in which everything was necessary and everything perfect. These convictions formed the very foundation of the modern individual's optimism about culture.

History has proved these convictions erroneous. The human spirit is free to do evil as well as good, to destroy as well as to build. The power of destruction is not intrinsic to the structure of reality as its negative mode necessarily; rather it is a power of negation in the most primitive sense of the latter term. Evil is done, but there is no reason why it had to be done; it would have been possible to do good, but the good was not done. The facts prove that an individual often takes an evil road. Our age is aware of the reality of the deliberate destructiveness in the human spirit and our age is troubled to its very depth. Therein lies its greatest opportunity: to grasp the truth by breaking away from the optimism of the modern mind.

The End of the Modern World, 1950, page 97

Demons

Demons may take possession of the human faculties if people do not answer for them with their conscience. We do not use the word "demons" as it is used in an ephemeral journalism. We are using the term in the precise sense given it by revelation. We mean spiritual beings who were created whole and good by God, but who fell away from him by electing for evil and who are bent on befouling his creation. These are the demons, then, who rule people once they have abdicated their responsibilities. Demons rule them through their apparently natural, but really human, contradictory instincts, through their apparently logical, but in truth, easily influenced reason. They rule them through the brutality committed by their helpless selfishness. If we reflect upon the events of the last years without either rationalistic or naturalistic prejudices, people's manner of conduct, their intellectual and psychological vagaries, speak to us with sufficient clarity of these things.

The modern world forgot the fact of demons because it had blinded itself by its revolutionary faith in autonomy. The modern world thought that a person could simply have power and rest secure in its exercise. Some kind of logic inherent in things forced them to behave in the realm of human freedom as dependably as they behaved in the realm of nature. This assumption is false. The moment that energy or matter or a natural form is grasped by an individual it receives a new character. No longer is it simply a part of nature; it has become part of the world surrounding the person, a world which is the person's own creation. The thing of nature becomes involved with, even partakes of, human freedom; in so doing it also partakes of human frailty. It has become ambivalent, carrying a potential for evil as well as good.

The End of the Modern World, pages 103–104 (1950)

Personality

Although human beings are intrinsically bound to nature in both body and spirit, as soon as they dispose of nature by coming to know nature they rise out of their natural milieu. They then place nature opposite themselves as something completely other. In the process of separating themselves from nature modern people underwent that second experience crucial for understanding the import of modern life. They underwent the experience of subjectivity.

The modern concept of the subjective is as foreign to the medieval consciousness as is that of nature. Seeing nature as the sum, the ordering, and the unity of all things, medieval people could not conceive of nature as an autonomous All. Nature was the work of the sovereign God. Men and women, the subjects, being of the order of nature, were first the creatures of God and the stewards of God's will. With the new consciousness of self, however, which arose late in the Middle Ages and especially in the Renaissance, the individual became important to himself or herself. The "I" — particularly the "I" of the extraordinary, of genius — became the measure by which all human life was judged.

Subjectivity revealed itself most distinctly in the concept of personality. Conceived as that which most expressed the human, as flowering from roots intrinsic to itself, as shaped in its destiny through its own initiative, personality became — just as Nature had — something primary and absolute which could not be questioned or doubted. The great personality was looked upon as a person who had to be taken inevitably upon his or her own terms. Only in the light of his or her own unique personality might one dare to justify someone's actions. Ethical standards seemed relative when compared with those which genius deserved. This new measure for judging the human act in terms of personality was first applied to the extraordinary individual; it soon applied to humanity at large. An ethos based upon objective goodness and truth was discarded for an ethos based in the subjective where nobility and truthfulness to one's own self prevailed.

The End of the Modern World, pages 56–57 (1950)

Culture

As with personality, culture achieved a religious significance revealing the creative mystery of the world. Within culture the "world soul" became conscious of itself; within culture the individual found the complete cause of being. Goethe expressed the full conception in his *Zalmen Xenien* when he said, "Who possesses science and art, possesses religion as well."

When faced with the question, "In how many ways can being be?" the modern consciousness answered unhesitatingly, "The ways of being are threefold: in nature, in subjective personality, in culture." The three belonged together; they conditioned and perfected one another. They created a unified framework, a finality beyond which the individual could not venture. That triple unity needed no verification from any other source, nor did it permit the existence of any standard above itself.

The End of the Modern World, page 60 (1950)

Chaos

The wildernesses of nature have long been under the control of humans; nature as it exists round and about us obeys its master. Nature now, however, has emerged once again into history from the very depth of culture itself. Nature is rising up in that very form which subdued the wilderness — in the form of power itself. All the abysses of primeval ages yawn before us, all the wild, choking growth of the long-dead forests presses forward from this second wilderness, all the monsters of the desert wastes, all the horrors of darkness are once more upon us. We stand again before chaos, a chaos more dreadful than the first because most people go their own complacent ways without seeing, because scientifically educated men and woman everywhere deliver the speeches as always, because the machines are running on schedule and because the authorities function as usual.

The End of the Modern World, pages 111–112 (1950)

The Stakes

Could the events of the last decades have happened at the peak of a really true culture in Europe? This frightful destruction did not drop down from heaven; in truth it rose up out of hell! A culture marked by a true ordering could not have invented such incomprehensible systems of degradation and destruction. Monstrosities of such conscious design do not emerge from the calculations of a few degenerate people or of small groups of them; they come from processes of agitation and poisoning which have been long at work. What we call moral standards — responsibility, honor, sensitivity of conscience — do not vanish from humanity at large if people have not long been debilitated. These degradations could never have happened if its culture had been as supreme as the modern world thought. . . .

The awareness of what has happened to modern people and their world is growing, but whether it is growing rapidly enough to stem the diseases which threaten to engulf the entire earth — diseases exceeding the disaster of war — is a moot question. In any event, the bourgeois superstition of relying upon progress has been shattered. Many people now suspect that culture is not at all what the modern age thought it to be; many suspect that culture is not a realm of beautiful security but a game of dice. Its stakes are life and death, but nobody knows how the last die will be cast.

The End of the Modern World, pages 105–106 (1950)

Solitude

Where the whole life is determined by the community, man is robbed of his responsibility and his humanity. Personal life is stifled when communities take control of power, as has been so frighteningly proved in recent years. The whole existence is exposed to the public gaze, to be supervised and directed by public officials. Initiative is extinguished by the regulation of all forms of life, for a standard form is provided for everybody. Man loses the capacity to subsist in himself, he becomes just a cog in controlling mechanisms. Man needs the opposite polarity to community, namely, solitude, in which he comes to himself. Man's ego is not ready-made like the concretion of an animal; he has continually to make sure of himself, to challenge himself, to form himself. This happens in solitude.

This means not only that no one is there except myself; it indicates the possibility I enjoy of turning and coming to myself, of standing up to myself, examining myself, accepting responsibility, and giving direction. It is in solitude that a living center is established in a characteristic way. It cannot be localized in body, soul or spirit, yet it is an object of experience, since positive and organic radii converge upon it from all sides. You can never say it is here because it is immediately somewhere else, between the observer and what he is observing; for all that, it is there and it determines our mode of observation. It would seem to consist in different acts of relation, control and command which are continually building the unity of the soul's life. But the unity they seek to construct they can also destroy, for example, through specious forms of force and regimentation, unless these are already controlled by the living center, which is superior to them. Much might be said about this phenomenon of a center, how to sustain and deepen it as well as its dangers and its possible destruction. Solitude in any case is a necessity essential to it. Where a man lives entirely with others, he loses his center and becomes a mere element in other patterns.

Solitude, when properly experienced, may be seen as personal liberation. Its power and necessity increase with the stature of the individual, and he has all the greater need of it when his special talents are of an active sort. One condition of a healthy life is that this experience of solitude be constantly renewed, to some extent by every man and, in a representative sense, by certain individuals for all mankind. Solitude stirs awareness of his personality in a man caught up in a network of community relationships. It makes him conscious of his own center, which at times is the center of the world, that is the real world: not the mere complex of available objects, but of the reality in which these objects are experienced, known and accepted by the person in question. Then what has been said previously about the individual center is carried over into the whole of existence. The individual experiences his uniqueness, which can be neither replaced nor displaced. This has nothing to do with selfishness or self-aggrandizement; it is the foundation of man's being and worth — of the individual who, as a person, can never be a means to a further end and also of groups which, because they are human, can be formed only of persons. We have the obligation of penetrating into solitude, into the realm of "myself with myself alone," and it is often extremely difficult to do so, because it brings a man face to face with the forces and tension of his interior life, with the exigent demands of conscience, and again with that particular void which renders association with the self so arduous and even unbearable and makes any exterior activity which distracts from it a welcome relief. I say nothing of the temptation of self to exaggeration, illusion, fixation and obsession, about which pedagogy as well as psychology provides copious information.

Finally, genuine solitude can be achieved only in the presence of God. If this is forgotten, the attitude changes to one of autonomy or exaltation and it heralds a further decline.

Freedom, Grace, and Destiny, pages 41–44 (1948)

Love

If I am right in my conclusions about the coming world, the Old Testament will take on a new significance. The Old Testament reveals the living God who smashes the mythical bonds of the earth, who casts down the powers and the pagan rulers of life; it shows us the person of faith who is obedient to the acts of God according to the terms of the covenant. These Old Testament truths will grow in meaning and import. The stronger the demonic powers the more crucial will be that victory over the world realized in freedom and through faith. It will be realized in the harmony between a person's freedom freely returned to God from whose own creative freedom it was gained. This will make possible not only effective action but even action itself. It is a strange thing that we should glimpse this holy way, this divine possibility, rising out of the very midst of universal power as it increases day by day.

This free union of the human person with the Absolute through unconditional freedom will enable the faithful to stand firm — God-centered — even though placeless and unprotected. It will enable human beings to enter into an immediate relationship with God which will cut through all force and danger. It will permit them to remain vital persons within the mounting loneliness of the future, a loneliness experienced in the very midst of the great body of people and all their organizations.

If we understand the eschatological text of Holy Writ correctly, trust and courage will totally form the character of the last age. The surrounding "Christian" culture and the traditions supported by it will lose their effectiveness. That loss will belong to the danger given by scandal, that danger of which it is said: "It will, if possible, deceive even the elect" (Matthew 24:24).

Loneliness in faith will be terrible. Love will disappear from the face of the public world, but the more precious will that love be which flows from one lonely person to another, involving a courage of heart born from the immediacy of the love of God as it was made known in Christ.

Perhaps an individual will come to experience this love anew, to taste the sovereignty of its origin, to know its independence of the world, to sense the mystery of its final *why?* Perhaps love will achieve an intimacy and harmony never known to this day. Perhaps it will gain what lies hidden in the key words of the providential message of Jesus, that things are transformed for those who make God's will for his kingdom their first concern (Matthew 6:33).

These eschatological conditions will show themselves, it seems to me, in the religious temper of the future. With these words I proclaim no facile apocalyptic. No one has the right to say that the end is here, for Christ himself has declared that only the Father knows the day and the hour (Matthew 24:36). If we speak here of the nearness of the end, we do not mean nearness in the sense of time, but nearness as it pertains to the essence of the end, for in essence everyone's existence is now nearing an absolute decision. Each and every consequence of that decision bears within it the greatest potentiality and the most extreme danger.

The End of the Modern World, pages 131–133 (1950)

Values

All life that is determined by spiritual factors has one essential postulate, namely, a submission to truth, the will to do justice to the nature of things. Only on this basis does the eye see correctly, the action retain its proper order and the work get done as it ought to be. Should this condition be absent, everything in the end goes wrong. But there is in man a factor that wants dominion, not obedience — not merely that dominion which is compatible with obedience to the Lord of creation but absolute power over the world, a dictatorship. This desire penetrates everywhere and it may therefore happen that an immense amount of knowledge, power and achievement, a creation of fantastic dimensions, is accumulated and yet the whole of it is wrong at its inner center. Indeed, this does actually happen. Modern man feels — consciously, if he is alive to it, or in the shape of a profound malaise, if he is not — that he is being damaged in every respect, in body and soul, in heart and spirit. He feels that the principles which explain life are not there, that relations between individual men are untrustworthy, that words are empty and his work is out of tune. He has a growing sense of being lost.

      This is no cultural pessimism and no romanticism but straightforward truth, and it would be very foolish to accept it as inevitable. Man cannot make further progress without asking what are the preconditions of the right kind of life. Since World War I there has been a marked shrinkage in the field of man's existence; it has become capable of supervision, and everywhere it calls for planning. But this planning signifies not merely that political, economic and sociological resources shall be established and used in the right manner but also that men shall inquire what are the essential conditions of this proper life. The first of these is found in the primary truth that man is indeed capable, as the image of God, of ruling the world, but in submission to the Lord of all created being (Genesis 1:26). Modern autonomy theories argue that notions like sovereignty over the world, providence, the judgment of good and evil and the establishment of moral values were formerly accepted as prerogatives of the Supreme Being but pass now to man, this world and this earth. "God" was once necessary because man was not yet mature. He was the form in which man, still in his infancy, beheld his own power; that was the only way in which man could then shoulder his power. Man has now grown up and become adult, and "God" is simply the obstacle on the path to complete self-realization. But what again if this be more illusion and presumption? What if God really remains God and man continues to be man?

      Further, it is not a question of a metaphysical theory out of all contact with real being but of the basic conditions for our actual human existence, conditions which permeate it even to the simplest details of everyday life. From these proceed the decision about the ultimate rightness and wrongness of everything, about good and evil in the widest sense. They again provide us with an answer to the question raised above. Revelation is the event in which God reveals himself and, at the same time, the situation of the world. It is at once judgment and also grace and a new beginning. Our attitude toward it is decision pure and simple because of our power of genuine freedom. But the freedom disappears as soon as our dominion over the world is not in its proper place and proportion.

The Purpose of Life

The purpose of life may be described as the realization of values. The word is not employed in an idealistic sense but to express the meaning of existence. Value is what makes a being worthy to exist and an action worth performing. The value attaches to the being itself as its essential and significant content; it also transcends it as the standard by which it is measured. Finally, value denotes the creative thought of God which establishes the essence and significance of the being. To speak of values is thus a shortened way of speaking about the particular character of being.

Every genuine value has its significance within itself. Strength is just strength and, because it is something primary, it cannot be derived from any other source. A man can realize it only out of itself, by acting strongly and growing strong. But the fact also remains that the man is essentially strong only when he is also just. Justice differs from strength, has its own significance, from which alone it can be put into practice. As soon as a man seeks power without justice, it is immediately altered. It becomes violence and brutality with a void of weakness inside it. Correspondingly, true justice preserves its character only when reinforced by courage, otherwise it may drift into insecurity and indecision. Utility again is utility and it indicates that an action is directed towards a rational purpose related to human existence. It becomes unfruitful, however, tiresome and finally unreasonable unless it also has a relation to the spontaneous development of life, to pure zest in growth and the joyfulness of existence. Similarly, these values become frivolous, trivial and wasteful if they drift from the order of intelligible ends. A careful analysis of wisdom would show that it requires to be related to the irrational and even to folly since otherwise it can be mere pedantry and lose touch with reality; that beauty can be superficial and destructive where it is not subject to a serious moral purpose; and that without the free flow of mercy justice changes into injustice, and so forth. Freedom consists in pure surrender to the value, but if this is not continually related to complementary values, it shuts itself up, as it were, and is made a prison.

Each value is a primary feature, established in itself. It is related also to other values and its character is preserved by this relationship. These values are themselves directed toward still further values so that we have a structure that makes itself felt in all activity. The Right, as an expression of what ought to be willed and done in the circumstances, is always complex and flexible. It is a balance that must constantly be readjusted to concrete reality if the whole structure is to avoid being hardened. The same is true of the various stages and levels of value within the universe. Animate being, for example, presupposes inanimate being. Man, in his biological capacity, rests everywhere upon the realm of inorganic existence. On the other hand, it is equally clear that the final conclusions of inanimate being are drawn only in the animate world. Mechanism, for instance, realizes its fuller possibilities in the organic world, which is essentially higher and different. Correspondingly, the spiritual factor has a continually changing relation to the vital element: an ethical attitude always presupposes biological potentialities. On the other hand, man's health, quite different from that of an animal, finds its last safeguard in the ethical order, to wit, man's responsibility for his existence. These glimpses suggest the vision of a whole, of a realm of values as the reflection of the significant content of the world, from which alone each value derives its truth. The question remains whether this realm of values can establish its unity from itself alone.

The world which finds its center in man has its orientation toward God. A man with keen eyes for reality [Blaise Pascal] has said that "man infinitely transcends man." Man soars above his own level and does not fully realize himself until he is in contact with God. In a certain sense this is also valid of the world. The self-sufficient world, postulated by some modern thinkers, does not exist; it was a postulate of revolt. What does exist is the world related to God through man. Man, therefore, in Augustine's memorable phrase, is by his very essence a searcher, and in man the world also is searching. The only realization of values which leads to freedom includes this knowledge and recognition. Yet, unaided, this quest does not reach its goal because of the confusion in which it is enshrouded, along with the human existence from which it proceeds. In consequence, it requires revelation and redemption, and it discovers the way only in faith. Revelation, which proceeds from God's free will, shows the goal to which all values are directed and it therefore provides the final safeguard for human freedom.

Freedom, Grace, and Destiny, pages 86–90 (1948)

Grace

Encounters take place in the world in the most varied ways and they culminate in the great adventure of surrender to a man, an idea, a task. They are realized in the manifold relations of subordination and communion, friendship, love, exchange and creation. The essential and final encounter, the encounter which is decisive for salvation, rises above the world to its creator, God. This is the object continually sought in religious experience in general, but it cannot be realized adequately except where God himself has made it possible.

God does this normally not by means of an interior movement of the individual but historically, by way of revelation. In this he made an approach to man, appealed to him, and received him into a new I-Thou relationship, in which man is enabled for the first time to rise to the stature which God intended for him, that of God's own image and likeness, his representative in the world, and a lord himself under the divine Lordship. The whole process by which God has approached man with his free benevolence, spoken to him, raised him up to a special personal association with himself, and given him a vitality proceeding from God's very life — all this is grace, in the proper sense.

This was first achieved in Paradise — a concept that needs to be freed from certain shallow and unreal interpretations of recent date. Paradise is not the natural situation of man before he had awakened to spiritual awareness, and it is no projection of a child's mentality into the mythical "long ago and far away." It was an existence which rose from the fact that man stood in full and undisturbed contact with God. At the same time, this existence was put to the test. It had to be decided whether man would affirm and preserve this sacred association or deny and destroy it. Revelation tells us that the latter occurred, not through any intrinsically necessary passage from natural innocence to sophisticated guilt but because of disobedience to the Lord of the world. Man consequently fell from grace, and this apostasy went deep down into his innermost life. What was left was not the simple, natural man, sound in himself and fulfilled in his nature, wanting only a special association with God. Because God's ultimate design for man was achieved only in his encounter with God, man fell below the level of pure nature and became the complex creature that we discover today, a complex creature embraced by no single category, himself out of order and creating further disorder, in revolt against God and in contradiction with himself.

From that moment man shouldered the weight of history. Had he been abandoned to himself, this would have been disastrous and desperate, at once the consequence of and expiation for sin. Revelation tells us, however, that God turned toward the world a second time and addressed himself once again to man. This occurred in the history of salvation, which reached its culmination in Christ.

Through Christ God enters personally into history. Christ takes upon himself man's guilt and destiny. Though pure and holy, he experienced these himself. He made expiation for them through suffering, which is in fact the essence of this experience, but also through an external fate that grew out of his inner disposition, his being and activity. In Christ God encounters man, invites him to cross over to him, and gives him what is a precondition for making that passage. If man listens to God, an association of a novel sort comes into being. God pardons the man his guilt, reveals his hidden truth, assures him of his loving good will, and creates in him the beginning of a new life which develops in existence upon earth and one day will be fully manifested. This is grace in the Christian sense.

Its more exact significance cannot be summed up in a few words. To begin with, it is God's mercy as revealed in Christ, his attitude toward man, his love. This love is not based upon anything in man that renders him worthy of the divine love, since he is God's creature and owes to God both his nature and his existence. Its motive lies within itself; it is a free initiative, which wholly anticipates the being and rights of the object it concerns. The love of God is a creative love and it establishes man in significance and existence.

Not that man in himself has no being or value, as has been suggested by a radical school of theological thought. This tries to safeguard God's honor by cutting man out altogether, as it were, and making the divine love itself the object of God's love. But the true meaning of creation is precisely that man exists only because of God but at the same time really exists, established in genuine reality and with a genuine significance. This is the man whom God loves. How this is possible is a mystery but no absurdity. If God loves man, he does so in conformity with God's truth. The account of creation informs us that after man was created, "God saw all the things that He had made, and they were very good" (Genesis 1:31); very good not in their own right but because of God — and really so, and in God's eyes, who judges absolutely. He has given to man such a mode of being that the divine love for man conforms to divine truth. The whole of the process by which God has this intention, required for this kind of action; by which he decides to create a finite being that can be the object of divine love; and by which he loves this being in reality and truth and with a divine earnestness — all this is grace, a pure decision of divine bounty, which no external force can compel and no external right can claim.

This is beyond our power to conceive, even more so when God directs his love toward man after man has rebelled against him; this love is then a redeeming love. Under these altered circumstances we insist again that God's love for man cannot be based upon any intrinsic value in man because value, like being, is first conferred on man by God's creative love. Still less, more decidedly less, can man's own being and action establish a claim upon God's love, once he has disrupted this relation of encounter and lost grace. God's decision to continue to love the rebel in a new way was an initiative of Divine freedom at a deeper level, a redeeming love. This in its turn is a mystery but in no sense an absurdity, and in God's eyes this love for man is even more intelligible when it is redeeming love.

Grace is, further, the relationship to which God elevates man. God approaches man, gives himself to man, and enables man to receive him. God calls man but also draws him so that he can approach him (John 6:44). Man goes across from himself to God and this resignation enables him for the first time to enter into full possession of himself. Grace is this manner of existence founded on this relationship. It signifies a share in God but it is God who has made that share possible. It denotes a continuing reception of divine love through which the real self develops.

Grace, finally, is everything operated by the relation we have been describing: enlightenment of mind, the ordering and strengthening of the will in good action, the interior life of love and familiar intercourse with God, the sanctification of life — in short, the rebirth to that new manhood of which Paul in particular has spoken so frequently and with such emphasis.

Freedom, Grace, and Destiny, pages 124–128 (1948)

Part 2

Jesus Christ

Chapter 3

The Message of Salvation

Mystery and Revelation

To this day Christian faith glows from the warmth, security, and love of truth which burned in Jesus' soul. The vitality of the divine word in him is other than that which so stirred the prophets. The prophets cried: Thus speaks the Lord God! Jesus says: But *I* say unto you. . . . His word does not serve; it *is;* creative, activating force. The ardor with which Jesus lives the word he speaks gives it its vital fire. We believe in Christian teaching as it was brought to us, warm from the living person behind it, taking it for itself, it would no longer be the word God meant. Were we to apply a single statement of his directly, from "God" to hearer, it would cease to be Christian. Christ is not only Messenger, but also Message, "the Word" that we believe. What he says is what it is only because he says it; the Speaker whose speech is an act of self-revelation.

    Good. But then the question returns, more pressing than ever: Why aren't we permitted to warm ourselves in Christ's fire? Why mayn't we hear his message from him? Since he is the living truth of God, corporeal Epiphany of the hidden Creator, why aren't we permitted to see him for ourselves? Weren't the men and women of his day incomparably more privileged than we? What wouldn't we give to hear the accents of his voice, to see him cross a street? What immeasurable assurance it would be to catch his eyes and feel his power surge through us, to know with every cell of our being who he is? Why isn't this granted us? We must know.

    Did those who saw him really have an advantage over us? Was "hearing" then fundamentally different from what it is today? One thing makes us pause: if it was so advantageous to personal faith to see the Lord, why did those of his day fail to believe? For with the exception of a very small group (possibly no larger than that of his mother, the two Marys and John) they did fail. Apparently then, it is erroneous to think that Jesus' bodily presence necessarily overcame resistance to belief. It is equally erroneous to think that immediate enthusiasm can replace the real essentials of faith: obedience, effort, responsibility. What would God's visible light make easier the decision? The quitting of self for the things of God? Obedience? Surrender of soul? He who wishes to facilitate such things risks underestimating the earnestness of faith; he is prone to seek refuge from obedience in sensational religious "experience." Probably he also has false conception of what divine light itself is, humanly enough imagining it as an overpowering sensation straight from the realm of the religious rather than from that of simple Christian faith. If we suppose that direct contact with Jesus would have automatically eliminated the intrinsic risk and struggle that are the elements of genuine faith, we are far from comprehending the Master of souls. Never would he have permitted this. The person swept to him on a wave of enthusiasm would have to stand his test later. The unavoidable hour would surely come in which he would be forced to a fresh decision — without benefit of transport, in which he too would have to take the step from "the direct experience of Jesus" to faith in Jesus Christ, the incarnate Word and Messenger of God. Isn't this precisely what was demanded of the Apostles at the Lord's death, then at his Resurrection, and above all, at Pentecost?

What then *is* really the Incarnation? It is the fulfillment of revelation, in which the unknown God makes himself known, the remote God suddenly steps into human history. Incarnation is literally what the word says: the living, actual Word of God, the *Logos,* Son in whom all the mystery of the Father is gathered, becomes man through the Holy Ghost. Do we see the essential now? *Becomes man —* not "enters into" a man. The Heavenly One is translated to the earthly scene; the Remote One becomes temporal reality. "And he who sees me" need no longer guess; he "sees him who sent me" (John 12:45). The Hidden One steps out into the open in human form, identifying himself with the form, content and sensory realm of the Word made man. Here is no place for dialectics which see in Jesus a mere human suddenly, at a whim of God's, transformed into the living No and Nevertheless of the divine Word. Such "logic" is only a clumsy attempt to veil a secret disbelief; Christ was not really God's word in history; he couldn't have been God incarnate! No. Truth needs no mental acrobatics. He who hears Jesus' words hears God. Understanding is another question; it is possible to "hear, but not understand" (Mark 4:12).

Incarnation, the *"deus absconditus,"* hidden God revealed in flesh and blood — strange how this very self-revelation hides him from us! How difficult it is to accept as God's living messenger, as the long-awaited Messiah, this Son of Man whom we see eating, drinking, walking the streets, who is threatened by countless enemies, who *suffers*. How I am to recognize in this transient, already doomed figure the ultimate measure of being for all ages?

God speaking human words from human lips, speaking from a human destiny, opens eternal doors to us. To enter them is what is known as faith; it is to know too, who God really is: not the "absolute" but — let us dare the word — the "human" God. Precisely here lies our chief difficulty, in his humanity. God cannot be so! we protest. His flesh and blood is simultaneously revelation and veil. The tangible erects walls; that which makes revelation what it is also shapes our "stumbling block."

We know only too well how difficult it is to hear Christ solely through his messengers. And not only through those first inspired ones who had been his witnesses and whose words bore the power of the Holy Spirit, but through messengers of messengers, thousandfold removed — spokesmen, moreover, who are not always swept along by their own vital conviction, sometimes indeed little more than hired teachers. We know what an added difficulty it is that the sacred word has been worked over and over by the centuries, and not without endless controversy and hatred and resistance; that it has been dulled by usage, lamed by indifference, abused by greed and the thirst for power. On the other hand, it is a help to know that so many have given their minds and lives to it; that two thousand years of history have lived in it; that so much humanity vibrates in the divine tidings.

Doesn't Christian community mean helping one another to understand God's word? Haven't we all known some person who has made Christ's message clearer to us, has taught us to pattern our lives more truly after his? Who is not grateful to some personage of the past, whether a great mind or a great saint or anyone who has taken his faith seriously?

When we reflect a little we begin to wonder whether Christ's contemporaries really had such an advantage over us. Was faith easier when Jesus wandered through Galilee, or after Pentecost when St. Paul preached in the cities, or during the persecutions, when the endurance of the martyrs blazed triumphantly, or in the centuries of the great saints of the middle ages, or now? A hundred years or five hundred, how much do they affect the eternal truth of God? To believe means to grasp what is revealed by the spoken word, the historical figure — through the veil that covers them both. The initial revelation must have been wonderfully powerful, but often insurmountable, too, the question: who is that man? Then the first barrier fell, the barrier of God as a contemporary. After that he could be seen and interpreted only in retrospect, through the glowing experience of apostles stirred by the power of the Spirit. But the more this indirect revelation spread, the thicker, simultaneously, grew its veil, woven of the human weaknesses of its messengers and the directions and abuses of human history. The problem of the later-comers, that of excavating the living Son of God from sermon, book and example, from the sacred measures of divine worship, from the work of art, pious practice, custom and symbol, is difficult, certainly, but probably not more difficult than that of recognizing him in the son of a carpenter.

And the conclusion? Aren't we almost forced to conclude that faith's situation remains essentially the same? Always both are present: what reveals and what veils. Always the demands remain the same: that our desire for salvation meet the desire for our salvation voiced in the sacred word. Naturally, in the course of time much changes; at one period a specific obligation is easier, at another more difficult; but the essential demand remains unchanged: the hearer must discard the familiar ground of human experience and take the plunge into the unknown. Always he must lose his life in order to find it (Matthew 10:39). How this happens in each individual instance it is impossible to say. Fundamentally there is but one essential requirement: readiness on the part of the hearer to receive revelation. Something in him must keep constant watch, listening, straining for the reply to his unceasing *qui vive?* [Who goes there?] No longer may he find full satisfaction in this world; he must constantly be on the look-out for signs of the other. Then when one day that other actually presents itself, he will recognize it. The form of one approaching through a fog is at first ambiguous. It can be almost anyone. Only two will know him: he who loves him and he who hates him. God preserve us from the sharpsightedness that comes from hell. Let us keep to the keen perception of love, even if it is only that of beginning of love; keep our desire to love one day with heart and soul for the coming of God's Son into our lives. Then when he does come, we shall recognize him. There is no rule for the manner of his coming, nor for the hour. It may be that the profoundest presentation has nothing to say to us, whereas a simple admonition or the magnanimity of a human heart may bring light. It can come instantly, but it may take years of waiting and perseverance in obscurity. Only persevere in the truth! It is better to bear uncertainty than to talk oneself into a decision that has no permanence. Genuine readiness already contains the seed of faith; untruth, on the other hand, that self-deception that pretends to views it does not really hold, and the violence with which we force ourselves to a creed which does not root in the heart, already contain the seeds of destruction.

This does not mean that doubts are already the beginning of a fall from faith. Questions can always arise to trouble us, particularly as they are usually afflictions of the heart that have assumed intellectual form. As long as our faith has not yet passed over to the beatific vision it will be constantly challenged — particularly in the glare of this over-enlightened all destructive age, bare of vision and unwarmed by the glow of experience, where it can survive only by the sheer force of fidelity. Moreover, there are profound questions that return after every supposed solution, mysteries whose intrinsic meanings, not solved but lived, increasingly clarify the faith of those who live them.

The Lord, pages 252 – 256 (1937)

Belief in Christ

Among the instructions that Jesus gives the Twelve before sending them out into the world are the following: "Do not think that I have come to send peace upon the earth; I have come to bring a sword, not peace. . . . He who loves father or mother more than me is not worthy of me. And he who does not take up his cross and follow me, is not worthy of me. He who finds his life will lose it, and he who loses his life for my sake, will find it" (Matthew 10:34 – 39).

Jesus' message is one of good will. He proclaims the Father's love and the advent of his kingdom. He calls people to the peace and harmony of life lived in the divine will, yet their first reaction is not union, but division. The more profoundly Christian a man becomes, the deeper the cleft between him and those who refuse to follow Christ — its exact measure proportionate to the depth of that refusal. The split runs right through the most intimate relationship, for genuine conversion is not a thing of natural disposition or historical development, but the most personal decision an individual can make. The one makes it, the other does not; hence, the possibility of schism between father and son, friend and friend, one member of a household and another. When it comes to a choice between domestic peace and Jesus, one must value Jesus higher, even higher than the most dearly beloved: father and mother, son and daughter, friend or love. This means cutting into the very core of life, and temptation presses us to preserve human ties and abandon Christ. But Jesus warns us: If you hold "life" fast, sacrificing me for it, you lose your own true life. If you let it go for my sake, you will find yourself in the heart of immeasurable reality.

Naturally this is difficult; it is the cross. And here we brush the heaviest mystery of Christianity, the inseparableness from Calvary. Ever since Christ walked the way of the cross, it stands firmly planted on every Christian's road, for every follower of Christ has his own personal cross. Nature revolts against it, wishing to "preserve" herself. She tries to go around it, but Jesus has said unequivocally, and his words are fundamental to Christianity: He who hangs on, body and soul, to "life" will lose it; he who surrenders his will to his cross will find it — once and forever in the immortal self that shares in the life of Christ.

On the last journey to Jerusalem, shortly before the Transfiguration, Jesus' words about the cross are repeated. Then, sharply focused, the new thought: "For what does it profit a man, if he gain the whole world, but suffer the loss of his own soul? Or what will a man give in exchange for his soul?" (Matthew 16:26)

This time the point plunges deeper. The dividing line does not run between one person and another, but between the believer, or one desirous of belief, and everything else! Between me and the world. Between me and myself. The lesson of the cross is the great lesson of self-surrender and self-conquest. Our meditations are approaching the passion of the Lord, so it is time that we turn to Christianity's profoundest, but also most difficult mystery.

Why did Jesus come? To add a new, higher value to those already existent? To reveal a new truth over and above existing truth, or a nobler nobility, or a new and more just order of society? No, he came to bring home the terrible fact that everything, great and small, noble and mean, the whole with all its parts — from the corporal to the spiritual, from the sexual to the highest creative urge of genius — is intrinsically corrupt. This does not deny the existence of individual worth. What is good remains good, and high aspirations will always remain high. Nevertheless, human existence *in toto* has fallen away from God. Christ did not come to renew this part or that, or to disclose greater human possibilities, but to open man's eyes to what the world and human life as an entity really is; to give him a point of departure from which he can begin all over with his scale of values and with himself. Jesus does not uncover hidden creative powers in man; he refers him to God, center and source of all power.

It is as if humanity were one of those enormous ocean liners that is a world in itself: apparatuses for the most varied purposes; collecting place for all kinds of passengers and crew with responsibilities and accomplishments, passions, tensions, struggles. Suddenly someone appears on board and says: What each of you is doing is important, and you are right to try to perfect your efforts. I can help you, but not by changing this or that on your ship. It is your course that is wrong; you are steering straight for destruction. . . .

Christ does not step into the row of great philosophers with a better philosophy, or of the moralists with a better morality, or of the religious geniuses to conduct man deeper into the mysteries of life. He came to tell us that our whole existence, with all its philosophy and ethics and religion, its economics, art and nature, is leading us away from God and into the shoals. He wants to help us swing the rudder back into the divine direction, and to give us the necessary strength to hold that course. Any other appreciation of Christ is worthless. If this is not valid, then every man for himself; let him choose whatever guide seems trustworthy, and possibly Goethe or Plato or Buddha is a better leader than what remains of a Jesus Christ whose central purpose and significance have been plucked from him.

Jesus actually is the rescue pilot who puts us back on the right course. It is with this in mind that we must interpret the words about winning the world at the loss of the essential, about losing life, personality, soul, in order to possess them anew and truly. They refer to faith and the imitation of Christ.

Faith means to see and to risk accepting Christ not only as the greatest teacher of truth that ever lived, but as Truth itself (John 16:6). Sacred reality begins with Jesus of Nazareth. If it were possible to annihilate him, the truth he taught would not continue to exist in spite of the loss of its noblest apostle, but *itself would cease to exist.* For he is the *Logos,* the source of Living Truth. He demands not only that we consent intellectually to the correctness of his proclamation — that would be only a beginning — but that we feel with all our natural instinct for right and wrong, with heart and soul and every cell of our being, its claims upon *us.* We must not forget: the whole ship is headed for disaster. It does not help to change from one side of it to the other or to replace this or that instrument. It is the course that must be altered. We must learn to take completely new bearings.

What does it mean, to be? Philosophy goes into the problem deeply, without changing being at all. Religion tells me that I have been created, that I am continuously receiving myself from divine hands, that I am free yet living from God's strength. Try to feel your way into this truth, and your whole attitude toward life will change. You will see yourself in an entirely new perspective. What once seemed self-understood becomes questionable. Where once you were indifferent, you become reverent; where self-confident, you learn to know "fear and trembling." But where formerly you felt abandoned, you will now feel secure, living as a child of the Creator-Father, and the knowledge that this is precisely what you are will alter the very taproot of your being. . . .

What does it mean to die? Physiology says the blood vessels harden or the organs cease to function. Philosophy speaks of the pathos of finite life condemned to aspire vainly to infinity. Faith defines death as the fruit of sin, and man as *peccator* (Romans 6:23). Death's arm is as long as sin's. One day for you too its consequences and death's disintegration will have to be drawn. It will become evident how peccant you are, and consequently moribund. Then all the protective screens so elaborately arranged between you and this fact will fall, and you will have to stand and face your judgment. But faith also adds, God is love, even though he allows sin to fulfill itself in death, and your Judge is the same as your Savior. If you were to reflect on this, over and over again until its truth was deep in your blood, wouldn't it make a fundamental difference in your attitude toward life, giving you a confidence the world does not have to give? Wouldn't it add a new earnestness and meaning to everything you do?

What precisely is this chain of acts and events that runs from our first hour to our last? The one says natural necessity; the other historical consequence; a third, something else. Faith says: It is Providence. The God who made you, saved you, and will one day place you in his light, also directs your life. What happens between birth and death is message, challenge, test, succor — all from his hands. It is not meant to be learned theoretically, but personally experienced and assimilated. Where this is so, aren't all things necessarily transfigured? What is the resultant attitude but faith?

Religion then! But there are so many, one might object; Christ is just another religious founder.

No; all other religions come from earth. True, God is present in the earth he created, and it is always God whom the various religions honor, but not in the supremacy of his absolute freedom. Earthly religions revere God's activity, the reflections of his power (more or less fragmentary, distorted) as they encounter it in a world that has turned away from him. They are inspired by the breath of the divine, but they exist apart from him; they are saturated with worldly influences, are formed, interpreted, colored by the historical situation of the moment. Such a religion does not save. It is itself a piece of "world," and he who wins the world loses his soul. Christ brings no "religion," but the message of the living God, who stands in opposition and contradiction to all things, "world religions" included. Faith understands this, for to believe does not mean to participate in one or the other religion, but: "Now this is everlasting life, that they may know thee, the only true God, and him whom thou hast sent, Jesus Christ" (John 17:3). Men are to accept Christ's tidings as the norm of their personal lives.

My attitudes toward things to be done may be various. One follows the principle of maximum profit with minimum effort. This is the clever or economical approach. I can also consider a specific task in the light of duty, the fulfillment of which places my life on a spiritual and moral level. Christ teaches neither greater cleverness nor a higher sense of duty; he says: Try to understand everything that comes into your life from the viewpoint of the Father's will. If I do, what happens? Then I continue to act in accordance with cleverness and utility, but under the eyes of God. I will also do things that seem foolish to the world, but are clever in eternity. I will continue to try to act ethically, to distinguish clearly between right and wrong and to live in increasing harmony with an increasingly dependable conscience. All this, however, I will do in the living presence of Christ, which will teach me to see things I never would have noticed alone. I will change my concepts and trouble my conscience — but for its good, stripping it of levity's self-confidence, of moral pride, and of the intellectual stiffness that results from too much principle-riding. With increasing delicacy of conscience will come a new firmness of purpose and a new energy (simultaneously protective and creative) for the interests of good.

Similarly, my attitude toward my neighbor may be ordered from various points of view: I can consider others' competition, and attempt to protect my interests from them. I can respect the personality of each. I can see them as co-sharers of destiny, responsible with me for much that is to come, and so on and so forth. Each of these attitudes has its place, but everything is changed once I understand what Christ is saying: You and those near you — through me you have become brothers and sisters, offspring of the same Father. His kingdom is to be realized in your relationship to each other. We have already spoken of the transformation that takes place when fellow citizens become brothers in Christ, when from the "you and me" of the world springs the Christian "we." Much could be said of the Christian's attitude toward destiny and all that it implies in the way of injustice, shock and tragedy: things with which no amount of worldly wisdom, fatalism or philosophy can cope — and preserve its integrity. This is possible only when some fixed point exists *outside* the world, and such a point cannot be created by man, but must be accepted from above (as we accept the tidings of divine Providence and his all-directing love). St. Paul words it in his epistle to the Romans (Chapter 8): "Now we know that for those who love God all things work together for good. . . ." This means an ever more complete exchange of natural security, self-confidence and self-righteousness, for confidence in God and his righteousness as it is voiced by Christ and the succession of his apostles.

Until a man makes this transposition he will have no peace. He will realize how the years of his life unroll, and ask himself vainly what remains. He will make moral efforts to improve, only to become either hopelessly perplexed or priggish. He will work, only to discover that nothing he can do stills his heart. He will study, only to progress little beyond vague probabilities — unless his intellectual watchfulness slackens, and he begins to accept possibility for truth or wishes for reality. He will fight, found, form this and that only to discover that millions have done the same before him and millions will continue to do so after he is gone, without shaping the constantly running sand for more than an instant. He will explore religion, only to founder in the questionableness of all he finds. The world is an entity. Everything in it conditions everything else. Everything is transitory. No single thing helps, because the world as a whole has fallen from grace. One quest alone has an absolute sense: that of the Archimedes point and lever which can lift the world back to God, and these are what Christ came to give.

One more point is important: our Christianity itself must constantly grow. The great revolution of faith is not a lump of reality fallen ready-made from heaven into our laps. It is a constant act of my individual heart and strength. I stand with all I am at the center of my faith, which means that I bring to it also those strands of my being which instinctively pull away from God. It is not as though I, the believer, stand on one side, the fallen world on the other. Actually faith must be realized within the reality of my being, with its full share of worldliness.

Woe to me if I say "I believe" and feel safe in that belief. For then I am already in danger of losing it (see 1 Corinthians 10: 12). Woe to me if I say: "I am a Christian" — possibly with a side-glance at others who in my opinion are not, or at an age that is not, or at a cultural tendency flowing in the opposite direction. Then my so-called Christianity threatens to become nothing but a religious form of self-affirmation. I "am" not a Christian; I am on the way of becoming one—if God will give me the strength. Christianity is nothing one can "have"; nor is it a platform from which to judge others. It is movement. I can become a Christian only as long as I am conscious of the possibility of falling away. The gravest danger is not failure of the will to accomplish a certain thing; with God's help I can always pull myself together and begin again. The real danger is that of becoming within myself unchristian, and it is greatest when my will is more sure of itself. I have absolutely no guarantee that I shall be privileged to remain a follower of Christ save in the manner of beginning, of being *en route,* of becoming, trusting, hoping and praying.

The Lord, pages 292–298 (1937)

The Beatitudes

In all Jesus says and does stalks a disturbing, antagonizing demand for a general revaluation. Healthy common sense says that wealth is blessing; blessing, the fullness of possessions; blessing, happiness and pleasure and fame. Our natural reaction to the Sermon on the Mount is one of distaste, and it is much better to face that distaste openly and try to overcome it than to unthinkingly accept Jesus' words as pious platitudes. That is the last thing they are. They come from heaven, but they shake, palpably, the foundations of earth.

The Sermon on the Mount is abused not only by those who resent all questioning of earth's supremacy, or by those who accept the words heedlessly, without making the slightest effort to realize in their own lives the thought behind them. All the mediocre men and women who attempt to justify their weakness to the strong demands of the world with the Beatitudes distort them shamefully, as do those wretched representatives of false piety who attempt to degrade the beauty and costliness of earth from "the Christian viewpoint."

Only he does not betray Christ's wonderful words from the mountainside, who keeps his eyes clear for the great and beautiful things of life, yet at the same time understands that even the best earth has to offer is paltry and stained and lost by comparison with that which comes from heaven.

In the Beatitudes something of celestial grandeur breaks through. They are no mere formulas of superior ethics, but tidings of sacred and supreme reality's entry into the world. They are the fanfare to that which St. Paul refers in the eighth chapter of his Roman epistle when he speaks of the growing glory of the children of God, and what the last chapters of the Apocalypse suggest in their reference to the new heaven and the new earth.

Here is something new, cosmic, incomparable to anything that has ever been. Jesus can express it only by turning all comprehensible values inside out. When a human being in the grip of divine power attempts to convey something of God's holy "otherness" he tries one earthly simile after another. In the end he discards them all as inadequate and says apparently wild and senseless things meant to startle the heart into feeling what lies beyond the reaches of the brain. Something of the kind takes place here: "Eye has not seen nor ear heard, nor has it entered into the heart of man, what God has prepared for those who love him" (1 Corinthians 2:9). They can be brought closer only by the overthrow of everything naturally comprehensible. Flung into a world of new logic, we are forced to make a genuine effort to understand.

After the Beatitudes, which dart like great jets of flame from the heat and power of the love that awaits us, there follows a row of instruction as to how, now that we have heard, we are to conduct our lives: "But I say to you who are listening: Love your enemies, do good to those who hate you. Bless those who curse you, pray for those who calumniate you."

Do we read correctly? It is enmity Jesus is discussing. What that is only he who has had a real enemy knows, he whose heart has burned with insult, he who has never been able to recover from the loss of all an enemy has destroyed. And now, that enemy is not only to be forgiven, but loved! No misunderstanding is possible: "And if you love those who love you, what merit have you? For even sinners love those who love them. And if you do good to those who do good to you, what merit have you? For even sinners do that. And if you lend to those from whom you hope to receive in return, what merit have you? For even sinners lend to sinners that they may get back as much in return. But love your enemies, and do good, and lend, not hoping for any return, and your reward shall be great, and you shall be children of the Most High, for he is kind toward the ungrateful and evil. Be merciful, therefore, even as your Father is merciful."

This is no longer mere justice or even goodness. It is no longer the voice of earthly reason that speaks. Something entirely different is demanded — the positive, heroic act of a bounty that can be acquired only from above, a divine generosity that is its own measure. And again: "And to him who strikes thee on the one cheek, offer the other also; and from him who takes away thy cloak, do not withhold thy tunic either. Give to everyone who asks of thee, and from him who takes away thy goods, ask no return. And even as you wish men to do to you, so also do you to them."

This certainly does not mean that one must behave like a weakling or surrender oneself to force. Rather, it means that man should extricate himself from the whole earthly business of defense and aggression, of blow and counterblow, of right and usurpation. He should emerge from the hue-and-cry of terrestrial forces and affiliations to share in the freedom that God alone has to give. The gist of the message lies in the words: ". . . and you shall be children of the Most High, for he is kind towards the ungrateful and evil."

Now we begin to see what Jesus is driving at: a bearing in our relationship to others that is no less than divinely free — not what law and order demand, but what true liberty gives. The measure of that liberty is love, the love of God.

Something of the superabundance of the mood is poured into the words: "Be merciful, therefore, even as your Father is merciful . . . give, and it shall be given to you; good measure, pressed down, shaken together, running over, shall they pour into your lap. For with what measure you measure, it shall be measured to you" (Luke 6:38).

To this we can only reply: But how can we possibly behave like God? And the question, which is really an observation, is sound. Alone we certainly cannot. But Christ does not stand by, a noble taskmaster, urging us to climb by ourselves heights far beyond our strength. What he desires for us is the supernatural life of the children of God. As long as we think from the worldly standpoint, this is of course out of our reach. But Christ says: "With men this is impossible, but with God all things are possible" (Matthew 19:26). He shows us that God not only demands this of us, but that he gives us his own understanding, his own strength, thus enabling us to accomplish his demands. We must accept this on faith. When the mind cries: But that is impossible! faith replies: It *is* possible! Our faith is "the victory that overcomes the world" (1 John 5:4).

Every day will close with the realization that we have failed. And still we dare not ignore the command. Ruefully we must place our failure at the feet of our Maker and begin again in the indomitable faith that we will succeed, because God himself gives us both the necessary will and the appointed way (Philippians 2:13).

The Lord, pages 73–75 (1937)

Mysterium Fidei

For centuries the descendants of Abraham have lived in Egypt. They have become a great people, originally highly esteemed by the Egyptians, then feared and hated. Now treated as bondsmen, they perform invaluable slave labor for Pharaoh, who in spite of Moses' command from God, refuses to let them go. Plague after plague descends upon the land, but Pharaoh stubbornly refuses to yield, till finally the Lord deals the terrible death-blow to all firstborn of man and beast, from the son of the ruler to that of the lowest slave-girl. God's own people are protected by the blood of the lamb on their gateposts commanded by Moses. A tide of grief sweeps the country; Pharaoh's will is broken, and he lets the Hebrews go.

In memory of this liberation and wondrous passage through the desert, the Pasch was celebrated annually, under strictest observation of the prescribed ritual, on the Friday before the great Easter Sabbath. The lamb was slaughtered in the early afternoon, and the meal began as soon as the first stars appeared in the heavens.

Originally it was eaten standing, in travelling-garb, as prescribed by Moses. Gradually the strict ceremony assumed the form of a prolonged and joyful feast, which the participants, as was customary on such occasions, ate reclining. During the past, the host blessed the wine-beaker and passed it around four times. After the first cup, a kind of *hors-d'oeuvre* was served; after the second, the host distributed unleavened bread and bitter herbs. The first part of the "Hallel," Song of Praise, was then recited, and the lamb consumed. After the meal the third and fourth beakers were mixed and blessed, and the second part of the Hallel ended the ceremony. Thus also Jesus celebrated the Passover with his disciples, who constituted the prescribed Pasch community. . . .

Matthew and Luke report: "And he said to them, 'I have greatly desired to eat this passover with you before I suffer; for I say to you that I will eat of it no more, until it has been fulfilled in the kingdom of God.' And having taken a cup, he gave thanks and said, 'Take this and share it among you; for I say to you that I will not drink of the fruit of the vine, until the kingdom of God comes.'

"And having taken bread, he gave thanks and broke, and gave it to them, saying, '(Take and eat). This is my body, which is being given for you; do this in remembrance of me'" (Luke 22:15 – 20; parentheses from Matthew 26:26).

St. Paul adds: "For as often as you shall eat this bread and drink the cup, you proclaim the death of the Lord, until he comes (1 Corinthians 11:26).

The chalice St. Luke mentions is the third beaker to make the rounds during the paschal rite. And according to one beautiful version, after the words "Drink ye all of this" the following were added "for the last time according to ancient custom." Then Christ takes the bread, blesses it, breaks it; and what he passes to them is no longer mere pieces of unleavened bread. He takes the chalice, blesses it; and what he hands them is no longer only the sacred drink-offering of the Pasch, but the mystery of the New Covenant just established. And all that takes place is not only the celebration of one high, fleeting hour; it is a sacred rite institutional for all time and constantly to be renewed until God's kingdom comes, and the Lord himself celebrates it again with his own in the unveiled glory of the new creation.

What has happened? For almost two thousand years men have prayed and probed and fought over the meaning of these words. They have become the sign of a community that is holier, more intimate than any other, but also occasion for profoundest schism. Hence, when we ask what they mean, let us first be clear as to how they should be taken. There is only one answer: literally. The words mean precisely what they say. Any attempt to understand them "spiritually" is disobedience and leads to disbelief. It is not our task to decide what they should mean in order to express "pure Christianity," but to accept them reverently as they stand, and to learn from them what Christian purity is. When Jesus spoke and acted as he did, he knew that all he said and did was of divine importance. He wished to be understood, and spoke accordingly. The disciples were no symbolists, neither were they nineteenth- or twentieth-century conceptualists, but simple fishermen much more inclined to take Jesus' words literally — if not with crude realism, as they had at Capharnaum — than spiritually. Even generally speaking, the man of antiquity was accustomed to perceiving and thinking through the evidence of his senses rather than abstractly. As to Christ's gestures, every detail of these men's lives was saturated with cult, and they were accustomed to reading truth from sign and symbol. Aware of all this, the Lord yet spoke and acted as he did.

Like the propitiatory sacrifices common in Egypt at the time of the original passover, the Pasch was a ritualistic ceremony for which a living creature was slaughtered, that its blood might be used to guard the people against destruction. So much then for the background of Jesus' act. He takes bread, gives thanks, praises God for the grace it contains, and blesses it, as shortly before he had blessed the meal. Then he breaks the bread and hands it to the disciples, as he had offered this or that partaker of the Pasch a tid-bit as token of friendship and community. "Take and eat; this is my body." Here on the same table the sacrificial lamb had lain, nourishment of the Old Testament. Those present cannot fail to understand Jesus' words in the same sense: ritualistically and mysteriously, but realistically nevertheless. Then, just as he had blessed and passed around the chalice of the Pasch, whose wine was reminiscent of the blood of sacrifice, he now says: "All of you drink of this; for this is my blood of the new covenant, which is being shed for many unto the forgiveness of sins." The old alliance had been in the blood of the paschal lamb and the blood of the sacrifice on Sinai; the new is in Christ's blood.

It is certain that the disciples did not grasp the full meaning of what their Lord had done. But it is equally certain that they did not interpret it merely as a symbol of community and surrender, or an act of commemoration and spiritual intervention, but rather along the lines of the first passover in Egypt, of the paschal feast they had just completed, and of the sacrificial rite celebrated day after day in their temples.

What had happened? Theology is constantly wrestling with the answer, yet one cannot avoid the feeling that this part of its effort has remained singularly unsuccessful. Perhaps it is just as well. In the holiest part of the Mass, in the midst of the transubstantiation, the Church herself rings out the words, *mysterium fidei!* Where is the impenetrability of divine mystery more apparent than here? Let us, too, respect it rather than attempt to explain. Leaving the "how" in all the density of its mystery, let us inquire only into the "what."

When a human being does something, his deed takes its place in history. Granted, it also bears a sense that outlives time — that by which it will be judged and transported into eternity. In one way, therefore, all action is permanent, elevated by the similarity of the individual to his Maker, and by the end to which God has assigned it. Generally speaking, however, human action is a part of time, and when its hour has passed, the act is also a thing of the past. With Jesus it was different. He was man and God in one, and what he did was the result not only of his human and temporal decision, but also of his divine and eternal will. Thus his action was not merely a part of transitory time, but existed simultaneously in eternity.

The earthly life of the Lord was drawing to a close; the treason had already been perpetuated. The rest was fulfillment of sacred destiny. Jesus' passion — which actually had started with the crisis in Galilee and was both temporal history and divine eternity — he now molded in liturgic rite. As he spoke over the bread and wine, he himself, the soon-to-be-slaughtered-one, with his love and his fate, *was* word and gesture. And not only once, in the house of Mark, but forever; for when the Lord and bearer of all power "in heaven and on earth" (Matthew 28:18) said "Do this for a commemoration of me," he was instituting something that was to remain to the end of time. Hence, as often as those authorized to do so say these words and make this gesture, the identical mystery takes place, and the passion, whose stand is in eternity, is caught and "brought down" in liturgical rite. In all truth may be said: This is his body, and his blood — this *is* Jesus Christ in his propitiatory dying! The liturgy is a commemoration; yes, but divine commemoration, not human imitation and memorial, not pious evoking of the past by a faithful congregation, but divine *in memoriam;* and fecund as only one other revealed act of the all-creative Father, that mystery of the infinitely holy passage: "In the beginning was the Word," eternal fruit of which is the living Son (John 1:1 – 2)).

What then is the Eucharist? It is Christ in his self-surrender, the eternal reality of the suffering and death of the Lord immortalized in a form that permits us to draw from it vitality for our spiritual life as concrete as food and drink from which we draw our physical strength. Let this stand as it is. Any attempt to "spiritualize" or "purify" it must destroy it. It is presumption and incredulity to try to fix the limits of the possible. God says what he wills, and what he wills, is. He alone "to the end" sets the form and measure of his love (John 13:1).

The institution of the Eucharist is also revelation. It reveals the true relation of the believer to his God: not before him, but in him. Among the farewell words that followed the sacred act we find: "I am the true vine, and my Father is the vine-dresser. Every branch in me that bears no fruit he will take away, and every branch that bears fruit he will cleanse, that it may bear more fruit. . . . As the branch cannot bear fruit of itself unless it remain on the vine, so neither can you unless you abide in me. I am the vine, you are the branches. He who abides in me, and I in him, he bears much fruit; for without me you can do nothing. If anyone does not abide in me, he shall be cast outside as the branch and wither; and they shall gather them up and cast them into the fire. . . . In this is my father glorified, that you may bear very much fruit. . . . As the Father has loved me, I also have loved you. . . . If you keep my commandments, you will abide in my love, as I also have kept my Father's commandments and abide in his love (John 15:1 – 10).

These are words that must scandalize and revolt those closed to the faith, but that to others are "words of everlasting life" (John 6:68; Mark 9:24).

In Luke's text there is a passage we must re-read: ". . . for I say to you that I will not drink of the fruit of the vine, until the kingdom of God comes" (22:18). We hear it echoed in the words of a man whose travelling companion and pupil Luke was, St. Paul: "For as often as you shall eat this bread and drink the cup, you proclaim the death of the Lord, until he comes" (1 Corinthians 11 – 26). Full of mystery, they too point to an hour that is to come. We cannot very well know what they mean, for they indicate the future. What a prophet says becomes clear only after it has been accomplished; until then it can only be reverently remembered and hopefully foreknown. These words will be clear only when the Lord has come. They suggest the heavenly banquet he will hold with his own when the kingdom has been established. There he will drink "the fruit of the vine" with them. It is the same mystery John once mentions when Jesus says that to him who believes he will come with his Father and "make our abode with him" (14:23). We are also reminded of similar parables of endless fulfillment in the Book of Revelation that follows. But there is little more to say. The promise must stand as it is; the heart alone can sense its meaning and wait for its realization.

The Lord, pages 368–373 (1937)

Chapter 4

Faith and Doubt

God's Patience

God is all-existing, almighty, perfect, eternal — the world is limited, imperfect, transitory. How can God care about the world? How could God have created it, or, having created it, continue to put up with it? Let us beware of giving too glib an answer. Let us give the question free rein. Let us feel the danger within it, the threatening darkness which it draws about our existence. Have we not at some time sat at a table where a tiny insect was running about and, in our annoyance, struck at it? What if God were to feel so toward us, toward the world which to him is as insignificant as the insect is to us! It is far from foolish to raise the question. God is no idyllic, good-natured, indulgent deity, but a power so mighty that all the terrors of the world are harmless in comparison. What is there about God that causes him to put up with us, not primarily with our sin, our rebellion, our disobedience, but with our strange, inferior form of existence? Why does he not simply wipe us off the earth? Do we not sense his patience, the mighty, deep, serene, forbearing, comprehensive patience which has sway over all things? Do we not recognize in it the self-revelation of God — that he is the very essence of patience? In that patience and in it alone do we have any safeguard for our existence, any guarantee for our confidence and security.

But our inquiry concerning God's patience has not yet been adequately, even properly made. Our question so far has been put as if it concerned the general rather than the particular. We should ask not about God's patience with humankind but, rather, with our own self. And we should ask with the urgency of personal involvement, in the confrontation of a dialogue that commits us — "Thy patience, Lord, with me!"

God prepared for the possibility of my existence through the unthinkably long evolution of the world. He desired that the world find its meaning in me as in no other. He laid the foundations of the motives and capacities of my being through long series of generations. He created me with the cooperation of my parents, and surrounded me with watchful care. He bore with my follies. He made me free to choose between good and evil. With his quiet glance, unwavering judgment and divine regard for freedom, he looked on while I went astray. He heard my resolutions — countless, always broken, renewed and eventually abandoned. He saw how I spent my time, my capacity for loving, my powers of action on all kinds of things, restless, unstable, constant in one thing only — my avoidance of what was truly important. . . . This could be continued at length, and whoever once starts this train of thought should follow it through and carry it into the inmost recesses of his or her heart.

All this God saw and bore with. What response does our heart make? Surely it cannot fail to be filled with the deepest concern lest God's patience be too severely tried. For it can, one day, come to an end, not because it would fail, but because, in God's truth, it had reached its limits. May it never come to this! In the Gospel we read the consoling account of Saint Peter's question to Jesus: "How oft shall my brother sin against me and I forgive him, until seven times?" And Jesus' answer: "I say unto you, not until seven times, but until seventy times seven." And if Jesus encourages us to forgive seventy times seven, here, in the midst of all the impatience of this transitory world, and expects us to be able to do it, how much more often than seventy times seven will the eternal Lord of Patience be able and willing to forgive us? God's patience is the complement of our weakness, and the justification of all our confidence.

We have said that we owe our very existence to God's patience. So, also, does all finite life. And it is by the power of this virtue that we are enabled to endure our own existence.

For what causes all the distress which is part and parcel of our destiny — privation, illness, enmity, hatred, unrewarding work, misfortune, loss — what makes it so hard to bear? It is so, though it need not be. Common sense and experience tell us that life is what it is, and that things happen as they do, whether we care to have it so or not. We see for ourselves that this is true. But we do not see that things must necessarily be as they are. Our heart protests against it, and foolish as the protest may appear, it is right. The questions that have to do with our own being — why must this happen to me? why do I have to be as I am? why do I have to exist at all? — receive no answer, for they are essentially questions which concern the meaning of finite life in general. I can see when a given cause operates a given result follows, but not why I have to be subjected to its operation; why such scanty means are allotted to me that I am unable to procure what I so greatly desire; why I should suffer this illness, this insufficiency of talent, this incapacity of feeling. This I do not see, and beyond that point only one thing can lead one on, namely, patience — patience which is the deepest possible acceptance of things as they are. Impatience is a protest against facts and, from the viewpoint of the world, there is no reason why the protest should not be raised. Why should I not seek compensation for this incomprehensible injustice by taking what has been denied me, and seeking to escape what has been imposed upon me? The answer comes from God alone. It is not, "God has willed it so," for that would arouse an even more vehement protest; it is, rather, that God acquiesced in these same restrictions. In doing what is expected of us, we are carrying on that mysterious limitation which God saw fit to impose upon himself.

    My greatest distress comes not from what happens to me, but from what I am — and the longer I live, the greater my misery grows. In children it is veiled, in youth offset by hope, in maturity compensated for by the confident assurance that one is making headway. Later, however, the sense of inadequacy grows insistent. The memory of things begun and never finished is ever with me. The petty, ugly things in my own nature force themselves on my attention — the fact that I am who I am and can never be another; the feeling of being closed up within myself never leaves me. In the midst of all my expenditures of energy, of all my endeavors, even during the hours of distraction, I am conscious of anxiety, of weariness, of skepticism. . . . That is my deepest distress. If one could only see all that frets and gnaws behind the miens of authority and sophistication, of cleverness and worldly knowledge, behind the planned projects and strenuous undertakings, behind even beauty and elegance, how could one bear it? In reality, one does not bear it, for what are all these diversions but efforts to escape facing the fact that one is what one is? And what are all these arts of adornment and disguise, of play and masquerade, but cunning efforts to slip out of one's self? And what the uses of vanity, titles and display but attempts to appear what one can never really be?

And then impermanence! Day after day passes — and the end of the week is always at hand; spring fades before one is wholly aware of its having come, hours of pleasure have a foretaste of what must follow; even in one's efforts towards self-improvement, one seems to hear a whisper — don't you remember, it was just like this last time. The faces of those about one change, one's own time is dying out. . . .

This waning of vitality, this continual ebbing of one's own being — who has not felt at times that a sudden termination of this life would be preferable to a slow drifting toward the end? What keeps one back from making an end of it? When this experience reaches a certain point, no ideal can stand against it, for ideals flourish in a warm heart and it is the heart that is now growing old. Neither can any mere moral law stand out against it, for moral laws, too, must be energized by strong vital currents, and one's vitality is now beginning to flag. Only loyalty to some unnameable ultimate upholds us — a sense of honor which forbids us to desert our post. Such slender ties, scanty strength, it would seem, should scarcely be put to too severe a test. In truth, however, they are, as it were, the innermost strands which hold being together, and they grow to be stronger than all that is burdensome, vexatious and destructive when they are recognized for what they really are — the human analogue of that eternal all-powerful strength which sustains the finite world — God's patience.

This is the innermost, the ultimate core: creature and creator conform in their patience with finite existence. Mysterious bond! Bleak, stark strength which supports all life! Nothing rich, nothing flourishing, nothing creative, nothing bold and venturesome without it.

Greatness sometimes stands out more clearly in simple things than in the more highly developed and complex ones. In patience, it seems to me, we come, at last, to that lowliest thing of all upon which, nevertheless, all earthly life depends. Those who are keenly aware of this truth have nothing more to lose, for they have already relinquished everything. It lies deeper than all else. It is the very heart of the matter.

The Faith and Modern Man, pages 26–32 (1944)

Faith and Doubt in the Stages of Life

Christian men and women are situated in life exactly as are all other human beings. Their bodies are made up of natural elements and are subject to natural laws. They live in the community of family and nation. They participate in the events of history, and share in the economic, scientific and artistic life of their days. Their dreams, thoughts, ethical motives, standards of right living, hopes of fulfillment, are like those of everybody else. But in their consciousness they have thoughts of another kind too — of the heavenly Father who created all things and guides people by his providential wisdom, thoughts of redemption and of a new, holy life which springs from it, which begins here on earth and finds its fulfillment in eternity. These thoughts do not derive from human knowledge and experience, at least not if they are taken in their proper sense. The truth that underlies them, the kind of mind they bespeak, the way of life to which they call, go back to one definite person — Jesus Christ. He claims to be the living revelation of the hidden God, the redeemer of the lost, the bringer of new life. . . . The Christian believer of whom we are speaking has, in some way, come upon Jesus Christ, either by steeping himself or herself in the sources which relate his history, or by having learned from others of his person and doctrine. They are convinced that Jesus Christ alone brings truth and salvation, that he alone sheds light upon the riddle of existence, that by his spirit alone can moral problems be solved, that he alone affords a final refuge to the human heart.

    The lives of such men and women consist of a whole in which two worlds intermingle — the natural life with its realities, and everything which Christ makes known of truth and wisdom, and the strength which he imparts. This unity let us call simply the Faith. It constitutes a very highly organized, unified life — if it really is what it claims to be, the highest life of all. It comprehends ideas, values, powers, has strong purpose, and provides a certainty beyond any other certainty. At the same time, like every other highly organized life, it is extremely vulnerable — vulnerable, indeed, in a very special way. When we consider how the gospel of Christ places a person under God's judgment, how it demands of that person a change of heart, how it requires him or her to give up much to which human nature clings for some distant goal, it is clear from the start that these changes cannot come about simply as the result of almost automatic development, but only through decisions and conquests, continually renewed. Since faith is life itself, life in the fullest sense, it must undergo repeated crises, crises which concern not merely a single part of a person's life, but their whole nature — their mind and all their potentialities. . . .

Much more could be added on this subject; but this much probably has been made clear — that crises in faith are not simple matters. Only rarely are they concerned with uncertainties in understanding — the interpretation of this or that point of Christian doctrine, or this or that passage of scripture. Questions of this character can be readily disposed of. But usually, as the whole nature of the situation shows, they concern something quite different. When one has discussed these things with many people, one soon notices that the arguments put forward are in no proportion to the conclusions drawn from them. They are, for the most part, characterized by a peculiar overemphasis, passion or bitterness or defiance, which points to something deeper than the reasons that are advanced — all the more so since the language which the objector uses is generally that of mere intellectual discussion, in which deep personal experience has no part. Doubts of faith almost always signify inner shifts of position, and the person whose religious life is at stake must recognize this fact — as must also those who have the responsibility for helping such persons.

The church says that people so afflicted may not set aside their faith, even for the time being. The ruling, in individual cases, may be felt as very severe, but it is right. It is based on the conviction that faith proceeds primarily not from human beings, but from God, whose power helps them to see as far into the question as is necessary and still to remain so closely bound to God that they will be able to persevere. Then, too, the ruling speaks from the knowledge that humans believe not merely with their intellect — that part of their nature which doubt seizes upon — but with their whole living being, so that they may place the center of gravity of their faith deeper, or at another point, and endure the difficulty until it solves itself. However, when doubt has penetrated so deeply that conscience can no longer give assent, the situation changes. Here also one can only advise that a person take no rash steps to destroy the bonds which hold together the deepest meaning of life. There is a virtue which is of the utmost importance in the business of living, namely patience, and here it is particularly called for.

There are two sides of the relation of a person's heart to God. On the one side is longing for God, longing for his sacred truth. But on the other side is aversion, distrust, irritation, revolt. It is this twofold aspect which makes religious doubt dangerous. The moving force in the doubt is hostility toward God. This we need to know. Therefore, in any wrestling with doubt, one must resort to prayer. The most effective kind of prayer is that in which we place ourselves, in our hearts, before God, relinquishing all resistance, letting go of all secret irritation, opening ourselves to the truth, to God's holy mystery, saying over and over again, "I desire truth, I am ready to receive it, even this truth which causes me such concern, if it be the truth. Give me light to know it, and to see how it bears on me."

The Meaning of Old Age

What . . . is the meaning of old age? This can best be determined by proceeding from the most important element in the preceding period — the experience of reality. In old age something special happens to reality. Its hardness is softened by the experience of transitoriness. Persons who once seemed indispensable die. One after another disappears — parents, teachers, onetime superiors first, contemporaries next. One has the feeling that a former generation has come to an end and that the following, one's own, is beginning to crumble. Many enterprises one has seen collapse, many organizations break down. One has lived to see the end of trends and fashions and standards of values. Concepts of what is right and fitting that had appeared unshakable and part of existence have lost their validity. These impressions will be particularly strong in a period of historic upheaval, all the more so if the formative years belonged to the period preceding revolutionary change. Reality then becomes questionable — not as in youth, when time seems endless, but rather because now reality has been found not to be as real as it appeared in the realistic period of mature life. The view of things widens out. Under the pressure of reality, a person was limited to the present moment. But toward the end the whole comes again into view. As in autumn, when the leaves fall from the trees, the view expands, and one is conscious of wide space. Reality engages the will in what is at the moment to be sought, done, mastered. But as the years go on one learns to loosen one's hold. The urgency of will begins to slacken. Detachment is the next phase, and a person's nature opens up to the whole, to a general view of existence.

Again we have reached a point that calls for decision, as, indeed, life continually calls for decision. Being is, in essence, ambiguous. It can always go right or left. The same feeling can turn out to be good or bad. The same virtue can work fruitfully or destructively. Just so here. The same detachment from reality, the loosening of one's hold on things, the sense of the unimportance of whether a thing is done this way or that, the accumulation of disappointments, the many renunciations of a long life may simply point to the end. Old age is that period of existence which life has been dreading all along — death spread out over years. That sense of the whole which more and more weighs upon us becomes the pitifulness of collective existence — the indifference of nature which kills as mercilessly as it gives life; the lack of consideration on the part of the persons around one who are put out by the presence of old people; the cruelty of the young who press ahead into life demanding space for themselves.

But this is not the true meaning of old age. That the will should lose its hold on things and on tasks generally, and that the hands be left free, should bring about a wider perspective in which that final thing, that real thing should become luminous. Out of that new condition grows a new form of belief. The danger in which aging men and women find themselves is that of capitulating to transitoriness, of having no more future, of living in their memories, of giving in to an existence which is ever more growing empty, of clinging to the fortuitous, of growing weak and tyrannical and at the same time powerless and helpless. The same danger threatens their religious life. There is a kind of skepticism possible only to the old — the cynicism of hopelessness which also affects their faith. It is the attitude in which mutability has conquered. In it nothingness rules. Death of body and heart has assumed spiritual form.

In direct opposition to this attitude stands the true faith of old age. It has cast aside the dreamy aloofness of childhood, renounced the endless demands of youth; it has experienced the transitory and seen how fleeting is human life, how questionable its works and its ways. Ever-changing life takes a new turn. Something final, something real has come through. At first it appears to be life itself, or, as we say half humorously, half wryly, life as it really is. But behind that looms something else — eternity. Beyond the mere drifting toward the end lies nothingness, dark, empty horror. To save themselves from it the old grasp at the nearest thing, this special food, that particular armchair, their bank account, their having the last word at home. But nothingness is not eternity. Before eternity stands death, but eternity itself is pure reality, endless fulfillment.

To be sure, it must continually be won anew through courage and struggle. But, the conquest made, there comes into existence a breadth, a quietness, a clarity of a new kind.

This struggle presses on into wisdom. Wisdom is insight into things as they are, and is acquired only when one is near the end. It cannot be taught; each must learn it for himself or herself through their own folly and out of the bitterness of their own end. It is the understanding of the relationship of the particular to the whole, and this understanding is achieved only when the whole comes into view — that is to say, at the end. It is the sense of what is important and unimportant, of proportion, of what is ultimately rewarding, and it is to be gained only when it is too late to change anything, but when there is still time for forgiveness, for contrition and for leaving everything in God's hands. Of this nature is the true faith of old people. Their attitude grows very simple, one might almost say childlike. Childishness is the ugly form of something which can be very beautiful. Second childhood, like first childhood, feels that all is one, that everything is under protection, that all will be well. Such faith is broad, understanding, tolerant. It is experience to the fullest — when it has humor in it. It is a wonderful thing, the humor of a religious person who carries everything into the boundless love of God, including the inadequate, the strange, the queer; who hopes for a solution when reason and effort can do no more, and who discerns a purpose where earnestness and zeal have long since given up hope of finding one.

The Faith and Modern Man, pages 114–115; 122–123; 130–134 (1944)

Adoration

A great and blessed mystery is adoration! In it we fulfill our ultimate obligation to God and at the same time safeguard our own soundness, for it is the instrument of truth. Adoration is not merely an act by which we reach out to knowledge of God, but a movement of a person's whole being. The very foundation, the pillar, the arch, the essence of all truth is this: God is God; a human being is a human being. Saint Paul, in his epistle to the Ephesians, makes use of a profoundly beautiful expression when he bids us "practice the truth in love" (4:15). We do this when we adore God.

Adoration is the safeguard of our mental health, of our inmost intellectual soundness. But what do we mean by that? Can the mind of a person fall ill? It can indeed. The body grows ill when it takes in injurious matter or disregards the laws of health. To recover, it must expel the poisonous matter and restore order. One becomes emotionally unbalanced by allowing the instincts to get out of hand, or by failing to exercise one's power of direction or control, thereby permitting a single idea or motive to operate to the exclusion of all others. If one is to recover, balance must be restored. But how can the mind fall ill? Mental illness, as it is called, is not really of the spirit, but of the nerves and states of feeling. Illness of the spirit finds entrance only insofar as it reaches the mind's seat of health, of soundness, namely, truth and justice. Our mind falls ill when we relinquish our hold on truth, not by lying — though human beings lie often (for in that case the injury to the spirit can be repaired by contrition and the renewal of good will) — but by an inward revolt from truth. True illness of the mind and spirit sets in when we no longer cherish truth but despise it, when we use it as a means to our own ends, when, in the depth of our soul, truth ceases to be to us the primary, the most important concern. In such a case, a person may not appear ill; indeed he or she may be functioning efficiently and successfully. But the order of that person's being is deranged. The scales with which such men and women measure are out of balance. They no longer distinguish between ends and means. They can no longer tell the destination from the way. They have lost the inner certainty of direction. They lack answers to those final questions — why? for what purpose? — and their whole being is affected.

 What has all this to do with adoration? In fact everything, for the men and women who worship God will never risk losing their balance. Whoever adores God in one's heart and mind and also, when the moment arises, in actual practice, is being truly protected. They may make many mistakes, they may be deeply bewildered and shaken, but in the last analysis the order and direction of their lives are secure.

 We do well to see this clearly and to act — really act — accordingly. But our resolve to practice adoration should not be simply one among many good resolutions as, for example, to keep one's word, or to do one's work properly. For here we are concerned with the very center and measure of being. Everything depends upon whether or not adoration has its place in our lives. Whenever we adore God, something happens within and about us. Things fall into true perspective. Vision sharpens. Much that troubles us rights itself. We distinguish better between the essential and the non-essential, the end and the means, the destination and the way. We discriminate more clearly between good and evil. The deceptions which affect daily life, the falsifications of standards are, to some extent at least, rectified.

As has been said, we must make a practice of adoration. The important thing is not to wait until obligation requires it, which might happen seldom enough; if we limit ourselves to such occasions, they would grow less and less frequent. Religious acts must be practiced if they are to grow into strong habits. God desires our adoration and we need it for our soul's health.

Whenever possible we should kneel. Kneeling is the adoration of the body. And in kneeling, we share the posture of the four-and-twenty elders who represent all creation in adoration before God. . . . Then we should be still, cast aside all unrest of body and mind, be quiet in our whole being.

At the moment of adoration we are there for God, and for God alone. This very detachment from the oppression of care, from the craving of the will and from fear is in itself adoration, and floods the soul with truth. Then say: God is here. I am before him as those forms in the vision, bowing down before his throne. I cannot see him, for everything here is still in the obscurity of time, still earthly. But I know by faith that he is here. He is God; I am his creature. He made me; in him I have my being.

. . . And now there is probably no need to write further. Those concerned must look up into the face of God — my God — and tell him what their heart bids them say. Then they will experience for themselves how really blessed and healing adoration is. So much that has been tormenting them subsides. So many anxieties show themselves to be groundless. Desires and fears become regulated. These men and women gather strength to meet the demands which life imposes upon them, are fortified at the very core of their being and take a firmer hold upon truth.

A person's adoration of God, here and now, with the limited vision possible in time, has a beauty all its own. It anticipates that stage when all will be clear and comprehensible. For whenever a human being adores God, the new creation breaks through. Is this not a wonderful thing to achieve? Wonderful, too, that a human being can give glory and honor to God even while the same God is permitting himself the appearance of weakness, and that a person may keep faith with him who, for the sake of truth, allows himself to be dishonored; to recognize that here and now God is worthy to receive glory and honor and power. Perhaps the greatest experience that can come to us is that we, transient beings, still caught in the confusion of this life, can give what is due to a God who is unintruding, can erect a throne for him in our own heart, and, for our own part at least, establish the true order of things.

The Faith and Modern Man, pages 10–14 (1944)

Part 3

The Church

Chapter 5

The Birth of the Church

The Scriptural Testimony

"Now Jesus, having come into the district of Caesarea Philippi, began to ask his disciples, saying, 'Who do men say the Son of Man is?'" He is told the various opinions in circulation, then asks who the disciples think he is, and Peter gives his historical answer, "Thou are the Christ, the Son of the living God." Jesus calls him blessed and entrusts to him the keys of the kingdom, names him the rock of his church, against which "the gates of hell" shall not prevail. We know the passage almost by heart, still there remains one point that we should try to see more clearly.

Here for the first time Jesus declares himself openly and unmistakably the Messiah, and simultaneously he speaks with equal definiteness of his coming death. The hour is also the decisive hour of the church. From now on three facts belong together: Jesus the Messiah, his death and his church. Before that hour the church did not exist, nor did she spring into being later as a result of historical development. Jesus himself founded her in the superabundance of his Messianic power.

The decision regarding the acceptance or rejection of his message has fallen; the Lord is on his way to death. The powers of evil have the upper hand, and the church will be attacked by them. Nevertheless, she will stand, rocklike. The two thoughts belong together, never to be separated.

To the reality of the church belong other passages which it might be well to mention here, among them Jesus' words about his disciples' mission: "He who hears you, hears me; and he who rejects you, rejects me . . . " (Luke 10:16). Something more than inspired men capable of inflaming hearts is being sent into the world; those being sent are delegates equipped with full powers, for they bear their high office with them. They are already "church."

Another time Jesus speaks of man's duty toward an erring brother. First one should tactfully speak to him alone. If he refuses to listen, one should approach him with one or two others, that the necessary warning gain weight. If he still remains refractory "appeal to the church" (*Ecclesia* — the word is still halfway between church and congregation and means, at least, a body with authority.) Then Christ continues, "but if he refuses even to hear the church, let him be to thee as the heathen and the publican" (Matthew 18:15 – 17).

At the Last Supper Jesus instigates the holy mystery of the eucharist already promised in Capharnaum (John 6). It is sacrifice and sacrament in one, mystery of the new community, heart of the new church's new covenant. Its consummation is her vital heartbeat (See Matthew 26; Acts 2:46).

After the Resurrection, recall the Lord's memorable questioning of Peter on the shore: Three times he asks him, "Simon, son of John, lovest thou me?" And three times, recalling his treachery, Peter replies, "Yes, Lord, thou knowest that I love thee." And each time he is commanded: "Feed my lambs," "Feed my lambs," "Feed my sheep" (John 21:15 – 16). That too is church. Once Jesus had said to Peter, "You are the rock;" then, "I have prayed for you, that your faith remain firm; when it is established, confirm your brothers" (Luke 22:32). Now he says, "Be the shepherd of lambs and sheep, of the whole world, which embraces both the weak and the strong." This is church again, founded on the unity of its fundament; constituted with one head and one leader. "Conceived" by the words spoken at Caesarea Philippi, the church was not born until Pentecost, when the Holy Spirit fused the individual believers in Christ into a single, determined body with a consciousness of its own, fully aware that it lived in Christ and Christ in it: the Corpus Christi. And immediately he whom the Lord has appointed its rock and its shepherd rises and speaks. His words are the first of the newborn church (1 Corinthians; Acts 2:14).

What does the church in Jesus's sense mean? The question is not easily answered, but that should not prevent us from trying;

we must constantly attempt to free ourselves from that false simplicity which is nothing but a mirage-like "comprehension" of conceptions that have become habitual. We want to experience the renewal of faith which comes when eyes are suddenly opened to the eternally new, the eternally fresh that is in Christ, and again we turn to the thought that has appeared so often in our meditations: the rejection of his message and the fundamental change in the course of his life that resulted. From that point on, God's continued will to salvation is forced up Golgotha. But what if the people had accepted the Lord? Would there have been a church then?

Our religious individualism is tempted to say No! The individual would then have turned to Jesus, would have been linked through him directly with the Father. Nothing would have stood between the soul and God as he is revealed in Christ. But this is not true. Let us recall "the greatest and the first commandment," which demands that the Christian love God with all his strength, and his neighbor as himself. Actually, the two commands are one; it is impossible to love God without loving your neighbor. Love is a stream that flows from God to me, from me to my neighbor (and not to one only, but to all), from my neighbor back to God. This is no longer individualism, but vital communalism. Jesus once warned against domination in any form: "But you are not to be called 'Rabbi'; for one is your Master (Christ), and all you are brothers" (Matthew 23:8 – 12). This is the beginning of the Christian "we." The faithful are to be bound to each other in mutual fraternity. They are the family of God, in which all are brothers and sisters and one with the Father. St. Paul completes the thought with great depth and beauty when he calls Christ "the firstborn among many brethren" (Romans 8:29). The communal spirit finds expression in the ethos of the Sermon on the Mount; in the Our Father it crystallizes into prayer.

Is it enough that everywhere the individual is bound through Christ to God and to his fellows in sacred "relationship"? Is the family of God the ultimate goal? We have already pointed out several times that Jesus addressed himself neither to the individual nor to humanity in general, but to a historical reality: the chosen people, with all that belonged to the term — vocation, guidance, loyalty and apostasy. This the people which was to speak the Yes, whose decision was to enter into the new existence of grace. What then would have stood firmly implanted in faith would again have been that specific people. Unlike the old natural covenant, the new would have been a covenant of spirit — in history, hence with a nation — the spiritual nation of the New Israel, "a chosen race, a royal priesthood, a holy nation."

[Here is] "church" again, historical reality and all that is bound to it in the way of destiny and responsibility. Hence the earnestness of the decision to be made by God's "family"; its new weight and dignity. This then was the church that was to stand at the heart of history, radiating, attracting, transfiguring. From every country, one after the other, a genuine community of blood was to rise, forming the one new spiritual nation. *Nation,* people — not group of individuals or heterogeneous mass, but folk, product of long history, vocation, guidance and destiny, and in its turn bearer of history, the history of God in the world. Ultimately, the number of mankind and of the new people of God was to be identical, for just as each racial and historical group was to be filled, one by one, with the spirit of the New Israel, so also unredeemed mankind was to be replaced by an all-inclusive family of the saved. But the arms of the church were to stretch still further, the established beginning made here was to permeate and transfigure the universe. Paul's Epistles to the Romans, Ephesians, Colossians speak of this mystery. "Church," then, was to be converted mankind in a transfigured world: the new creation born of the Holy Spirit.

Yet this would not have taken place in a burst of formless enthusiasm. Throughout the process, apostolic office and mission, power and obedience, differentiation between authorities, mystery and the sharing of mystery are not to be thought away: ordered whole, and in that order and completeness, true church. This is already made clear in the sending forth of the apostles before the decision has fallen. St. Paul compares the church to a body with many parts. He speaks of the many graces or "varieties of gifts" in the one Spirit, of the manifold expressions coming from the one organic unity (see 1 Corinthians). It is the same thought that Jesus expresses in the parable of the one vine and the many branches in John 15.

And there is still another image, this time from the prophecies, that of the Messianic Kingdom of New Jerusalem (Isaiah 65:17). Initially the actual city of Jerusalem is meant; it is then transfigured to the holy City of the Messiah. St. Paul also speaks of "that Jerusalem which is above," the city freed by grace and faith, mother whose children are born into freedom, not into the slavery of the flesh as were the former children (Galatians 4:21 – 26). And finally in the Apocalypse the radiant Jerusalem, heavenly city, unit of sacred mankind (21:9 – 27). Here it is again, church, the great congregation, spiritually ordered community life, as a powerful historical reality. In the words of the Apocalypse the metaphor of the city receives its ultimate impressiveness.

Is the church we know today the same she would have been in the accepted kingdom of God? Church was to exist; Jesus wanted no individualistic piety. He wanted the *Ecclesia* based on confidence, freedom and love. This does not mean a bodiless "spiritual church," nor does it mean a purely pneumatological church incapable of taking its place in history. Always there would have been organization and order, differences of office and authority, leaders and led, ecclesiastic and layman, authoritative teaching and obedient acceptance — but in freedom, love and trust. Unfortunately, the second Fall occurred — rejection of God's Son — and ever since, the church too has borne the marks: danger of mistaking sacred order for "law," danger of abusing it.

What then is the present church? The fullness of grace functioning in history. Mystery of that union into which God, through Christ, draws all creation. Family of the children of God assembled about Christ, the firstborn. Beginning of the new holy people. Foundation of the Holy City once to be revealed. And simultaneous with all her graces are her dangers: danger of dominating, danger of "the law." When we speak of the church, we cannot ignore the fact of Christ's rejection, which never should have been. We cannot ignore the terrible means by which we came to salvation; the consequences have penetrated deep into existence. Accordingly, we have neither the church we might have had, nor the church we one day will have. We have the church scarred by that most tragic of all decisions.

Nevertheless, she is and remains the mystery of the new creation, Mother constantly bearing and rebearing new life. Between Christ and herself flows the mystery of love. She is Bride. When St. Paul, in his letter to the Ephesians, speaks of the mystery of Christian marriage, he grounds it in the greater nuptial mystery of Christ and his church. (The image should not be used lightly, for it is indeed a "high mystery" and renders the sacrament of human marriage only the more impenetrable.) The church is the Holy City of the Apocalypse, blazing in an unutterable mystery of beauty and love, when suddenly transformed into a shimmering Bride, she steps down to receive the Bridegroom.

All this exists, and with it the flaws, the abuses, the rigors. We have no choice but to accept the whole, as it is. The church is a mystery of faith and can be experienced only in love.

The Lord, pages 238–242 (1937)

Pentecost: The Event

It was characteristic of the life of Jesus that the result — if we may be permitted to use the word in dealing with so sacred a subject — was not visible during his earthly life. He was to remain the sower, others were to reap the harvest. He himself had said, "In this is the saying true that it is one man that sows and it is another that reaps. I have sent you to reap that in which you did not labor. Others have labored and you have entered into their labors." (John 4:37–38). That was also true of him. That which was to come forth from his prayer, his teaching, his actions and his suffering, lay beyond the tomb.

Everything was in the process of becoming — full of promise but without visible form. The future apostles were ready, but in terror of their foes. Their memory recalled the words and deeds and fate of their Master, but they did not yet understand the true meaning and interrelation of these things. Their Master was everything to them, but they did not yet know who he really is, and their loyalty had not yet reached the point of triumphing over earthly things.

Therefore, after the death of Jesus, the disciples felt that they were in a state of expectancy. At the very last moment, in the deeply mysterious hour of his return to the Father, they asked, "Lord, wilt thou at this time restore again the kingdom of Israel?" (Acts 1:6) — the kingdom in which they (we may add this with reference to Matthew 18:1 and 20:20) — would sit upon the "twelve thrones," of which Jesus had spoken in a very different sense (Matthew 19:28). So they waited.

And now the book of Acts tells us:

> And when the days of the Pentecost were accomplished, they all were together in one place; and suddenly there came a sound from heaven, as of a mighty wind coming, and it filled the whole house where they were sitting. And there appeared to them parted tongues as it were of fire, and it sat on every one of them. And they were all filled with the Holy Ghost and they began to

speak with diverse tongues, according as the Holy Ghost gave them to speak. (Acts 2:1 – 4)

The occurrence was observed; a crowd gathered in front of the house:

Now there were dwelling at Jerusalem Jews, devout men, out of every nation under heaven. And when this was noised abroad, the multitude came together and were confounded in mind, because every man heard them speak in his own tongue. And they were all amazed, and wondered, saying, "Behold, are not all these that speak Galileans? And how have we heard every man our own tongue wherein we were born?". . . and they were all astonished and wondered, saying one to another, "What does this mean?" But others, mocking, said, "These men are full of new wine" (Acts 2:5 – 8, 12 – 13).

The time had come for the first testimony:

But Peter standing up with the eleven, lifted up his voice and spoke to them: "Ye men of Judea, and all you that dwell in Jerusalem, be this known to you, and with your ears receive my words. For these are not drunk, as you suppose, seeing it is but the third hour of the day; but this is that which was spoken of by the prophet Joel: And it shall come to pass in the last days (saith the Lord) I will pour out of my Spirit upon all flesh, and your sons and your daughters shall prophesy (Acts 2:14 – 18).

And he continued:

Men of Israel, hear these words: Jesus of Nazareth, a man approved of God among you by miracles and wonders and signs, which God did by him, in the midst of you, as you also know; this same man delivered up, by the determinate counsel and foreknowledge of God, you by the hands of wicked men have crucified and slain. . . . Therefore let all the house of Israel know most certainly, that God has made both Lord and Christ this same Jesus, whom you have crucified (Acts 2:22 – 23, 36).

This was the first proclamation of the message, and it contained a sacred power:

When they had heard these things they had compunction in their heart and said to Peter and to the rest of the apostles, "What shall we do, men and brethren?" But Peter said to them, "Do penance and be baptized every one of you in the name of Jesus Christ for the remission of your sins, and you shall receive the gift of the Holy Ghost." . . . They therefore that received his word were baptized, and there were added in that day about three thousand souls (Acts 37–38, 41).

This was the event for which they had been waiting. And what was it that happened?

A mysterious power began its work. Its action is expressed by images taken from the elemental forces of nature: a flaming fire and a rushing wind. But the force itself is not a natural one, for we are told that the flames took the form of human tongues, and the rushing wind produced words; that is, it possessed mind and meaning.

In order to understand what was taking place we must turn to the Old Testament and see how the Spirit works here. The word "spirit" as used here does not mean reason, logic, calculation, but the religious spirit, *pneuma*. In this concept many ideas are combined: that activity which is invisible and yet so effective, the breath, the power and expression of life; then the great breath of the world, the wind, which we do not see — Jesus said to Nicodemus, "Thou knowest not whence it comes or whither it goeth" (John 3:8) — and yet it can fill the sails and shatter the trees; then the soul, which no man grasps or measures, and yet we live and act by it. All this is involved and points to something greater and more mysterious which comes directly from God: the Holy Spirit.

He brings it about that there shall be a man somewhere, whatever his origin may be — Isaias, or Jeremias, or Jonas — who becomes a prophet, capable of understanding the meaning of God's action in time, here and now, and who has the courage to step forward and to proclaim, "Thus says the Lord!" The Spirit awakens the leader in the events of sacred history, for instance, that immeasurably great man, Moses. He calls the hero who fights not for his own glory, but for the accomplishment of God's will, as did Gideon or David. He enlightens the judge who administers the law among God's people; again we think first of Moses or Josue, or the figures of the book of Judges. He inspires the artist who works for the adornment of the holy place, as in the vocation of Bezalel (Exodus 35:30 ff.). And all of this is done not by way of natural talent, but so that the power of God is revealed thereby.

The Spirit penetrates the inmost recesses of life. As the breath draws the air into the interior reaches of the body, so the power of God is drawn by the Spirit into a human being and transforms it.

Samuel said to Saul, "The Spirit of the Lord shall come upon thee . . . and thou shalt be changed into another man" (1 Samuel 10:6). The Spirit brings it about that a man grasps a truth which of himself he could not understand; that an attitude awakens within him which would otherwise be beyond his capacity; that he experiences a presence of God which he himself could not attain. This is the Spirit who operated on the occasion we described.

Let us disregard theory; let us look upon the phenomenon: What were these men who in the hour of Pentecost were seized and gave testimony, Peter and the eleven? What were they before this event? They were men whose conduct certainly does not give the impression of heroism. We are told explicitly that they sat behind closed doors, fearful that they might suffer the same fate as their Master (John 20:19). But now they stepped forth and spoke.

We must also remember the particular time in which this took place: the weeks of the great pilgrimage, during which Jerusalem swarmed with men of all nations, excitable as such crowds always are, humanly, religiously and politically. At any moment a spark could catch and fanatical rage could flare up against the followers of the man recently executed. It was a crowd such as this that the apostles confronted and to which they spoke: "Let all the house of Israel know most certainly that God has made both Lord and Christ this same Jesus whom you have crucified" (Acts 2:36). These were the same men who before this had hidden themselves in fear — and yet they were entirely different. This was the work of the Spirit.

Each spoke with compelling authority, not only as one who has had an experience might say to another: "It is so; I have experienced it." That would indeed be a kind of authority, but it would be the authority of one who had gained insight by natural means or who had endured suffering. This was different. This was an authority that did not admit of argument, one that must be obeyed or rejected.

But what were they saying as they addressed the crowd so authoritatively? What was the subject of their speech? It was Christ. And how did they speak of him? If we compare the relation of the Apostles to Christ before Pentecost with that which became manifest on this occasion we perceive a profound and intrinsic difference. Of course he had been their Master before. They accompanied him, listened to his words, observed what he did and how men behaved toward him. They were witnesses of everything, so that they could say later that no one could be an apostle who had not been with them from the beginning and hence was capable of speaking from experience (Acts 1:21ff.). But can we maintain that they understood him? To some extent, naturally, they did understand him. When he said that his disciples should avoid not only deeds but even words of hatred, should not merely pardon a limited number of times, but should always be ready to forgive — and the other things that he always taught them in regard to the proper attitude of children of God — then they understood the words in a general human sense. They also perceived the purity and selflessness of their Master, the power of helping and healing that proceeded from him, the atmosphere of stillness which enveloped him in spite of all the turmoil around him. But always he remained, as it were, ahead of them, beyond them. They were always approaching him from a distance — the distance of their Old Testament world and way of thinking.

After the Spirit had come upon them a mysterious change of position took place. Now they spoke from his point of view. He was no longer "before" them, he was "in" them. As they spoke, he was speaking. Later St. Paul would write about this "in" from deep personal experience. He was in Christ and Christ in him. "Now it is no longer I who live, but Christ lives in me" (Galatians 2:20). But there is more: When these twelve apostles speak, it is not as if a group of twelve men had the same experience and then each one stepped forward (Acts 2:14) and stated: "I also vouch for this; I corroborate what our spokesman is saying." When we speak of "the twelve" this is not merely a number — twelve instead of twenty or a hundred — but a symbol, namely the twelve tribes of Israel, who must then be re-interpreted as the twelve tribes of the new holy nation, that is, the totality of the believers. These twelve, therefore, are not just a number, but a figure.

How close and strong this unity is we may perceive by considering an event which followed soon after and had important consequences. Some time after the occurrences on the day of Pentecost, Paul went from Jerusalem to Damascus in order to carry on the persecution there (Acts 9:2 ff.). On the way the Lord met him and Paul collapsed on the road. The meeting was both a defeat and a vocation: Jesus turned the persecutor into his servant and apostle. Immediately Paul began to teach, and he did it with a power which still rings in his Epistles. If anyone had been capable of acting alone, merely as a result of his vocation by Jesus, then it was Paul. Humanly speaking, he must have been strongly tempted to do so, for the original apostles did not make things easy for him. When they chose Matthias they had made the rule that only one who had been with Jesus from the beginning could become an apostle (Acts 1:21). Paul had never seen Jesus in his earthly form; therefore, they felt that this additional apostle was somewhat irregular — quite apart from the fact that it was he who had so deeply disturbed the pleasant peace of the original community. How great was Paul's temptation to say, "I do not need you. I was called by the Lord himself." And at the beginning of the Epistle to the Galatians he does call himself most emphatically, "Paul, an apostle, not of men, neither by man, but by Jesus Christ, and God the Father, who raised him from the dead" (Galatians 1:1). The excitement of Paul's first experience had lengthy repercussions. We need only read in the second Epistle to the Corinthians how he speaks of the difficulties of his apostolic life, or note the tone in which the Epistle to the Galatians speaks of James and Peter and John "who are regarded as the pillars" (2:9). But he, who could say of himself "I have labored more abundantly than all (the others)" (1 Corinthians 15:10) went to Jerusalem and gave the apostles an account of what he had done and accepted their decision as to what he might maintain and what not (Acts 21:15 – 26; Galatians 2:1 – 10).

All this means that "the twelve" were not merely a group of men which might just as well have been larger or smaller; they were — together with those who gathered around them — a figure, a whole, an organism, which stood in objective validity and authority. They were — the church!

The Church of the Lord, pages 29 – 36 (1965)

Pentecost: The Consequences

If we consider all this, how shall we express what happened on the day of Pentecost? At first the obvious answer would seem to be: the church was founded. But this would not correctly express the occurrence which the book of Acts relates. There was something which preceded. Jesus chose the twelve and entrusted his work to them; he spoke to Peter of the rock on which he intended to build his church. He made the eucharist the core and the central mystery of the church that was to be, apart from the fact that he lived with them throughout this time, spoke to them, wove his sacred form into their minds and souls. But all this was not an accomplishment but a preparation, a foundation and a germ. Then, on the day of Pentecost, the church was "born."

The church is not an invented and constructed institution, however wise and powerful, but a living being which has come forth from an occurrence that is both divine and human, the event of Pentecost. She lives on through time, in the process of becoming, like every living thing. She changes as everything in history changes with time and destiny and yet essentially she is always the same, and her inmost core is Christ.

This determines the way in which we must understand her. So long as we regard the church merely as an organization which serves definite purposes, as a governing body which is opposed to the freedom of the individual, as a federation of those who have the same views and attitudes in religious matters, we do not have the right relation to her. She is a living being, and our relation to her must itself be a vital one.

This is a subject which we must consider more carefully.

The living being of which we are speaking possesses a mighty power: According to the will of Christ it must leaven every period of history, penetrate into all corners of the earth and take hold of all nations (Matthew 28:19 ff.). It is of unshakable solidity, a solidity which is the power of truth. Jesus himself compares it to a building which he will erect on a rock foundation (Matthew 16:18). This motif of strength and solidity was marvelously developed by St. John in the Apocalypse. He unfolds in an impressive vision the image of the heavenly city (21:9 ff.). But at the same time the impression of rigidity that one associates with the image of a building, and the feeling of coldness that would be produced by the stones, is transformed into a thing of life as we read that the heavenly Jerusalem comes down from God "dressed as a bride adorned for her husband."

The concept of the church as a living being was most emphatically stated and worked out by that apostle who would perhaps have been most tempted and most able to fashion Christian existence into an immediate and individual relation to Christ, St. Paul. We have already spoken of this, and of the fact that he used the ancient concept of the *corpus*. "The body of the church," he says with forceful brevity (1 Corinthians 12:27; Colossians 1:18). He combines this concept with the idea of the spiritually transformed corporeality of the risen Christ. So he constructs the fruitful concept of the *corpus Christi mysticum* of which the believers are members (1 Corinthians 12:12 ff.).

Then St. Paul's image expands into cosmic dimensions. The Epistle to the Ephesians (1:23 ff.) and that to the Colossians (1:15 ff.) announce with visionary power that the "body of Christ," transformed by the Spirit in the Resurrection, shall take hold of the whole world and draw it into the unity of one life whose fullness is ordered and guided by the ruling power of the sacred Head.

The vital powers of this church are enormous. The individual persons are incorporated in it, yet each of these is also immediately related to Christ and has its own individuality. (1 Corinthians 12 ff.). Each one is a "member." We have already suggested a modern image: each one is a "cell" in this great living organism, carried, arranged and united by the molding force which proceeds from the sacred Head. The question arises how the individual life and personal dignity of each one is related to this mighty totality. The answer which follows immediately from the organic image would be that the individuality, the personal life and freedom of each one is not crushed by the vitalizing energy of the whole but on the contrary is emphasized and supported by it in order that what we call "life" may unfold. The passage of the Epistle to the Corinthians to which we have referred expresses it very clearly. The church is a church of persons and personalities.

Here an important phenomenon becomes clear — that of authority. That Christ gave to the church authority — that is, competence and power — is proved by words such as these:

> If thy brother shall offend against thee, go and rebuke him between thee and him alone. If he shall hear thee, thou shalt gain thy brother. And if he will not hear thee, take with thee one or two more, that in the mouth of two or three witnesses every word may stand. And if he will not hear them, tell the church. And if he will not hear the church, let him be to thee as the heathen and publican [that is, an enemy of the community]. Amen, I say to you, whatsoever you shall bind on earth, shall be bound also in heaven, and whatsoever you shall loose upon earth, shall be loosed also in heaven (Matthew 18:15 – 18).

At once the question arises: What is the nature of this authority — especially in view of the role which the church has sometimes had to play in history? Here again it is Jesus himself who gives a very clear answer. It is a competence and power not of lordship but of service. When the mother of the sons of Zebedee requested for them positions of honor in the kingdom of God, Jesus said,

> You know that the princes of the Gentiles lord it over them, and they that are the greater exercise power upon them. It shall not be so among you, but whosoever will be the greater among you let him be your minister, and he that will be first among you shall be your servant; even as the Son of Man is not come to be ministered unto, but to minister (Matthew 20:25-28).

These words indicate the difference between the use which "Gentile" rulers make of their power and that which God demands of those who have authority in the church.

In order to connect in the minds of the apostles an image of the exercise of authority for service — that is, an authority based on love and selflessness — with the memory of their last gathering before his death, he had, before instituting the great mystery of the church — the eucharist — washed their dusty feet. He performed the service of a slave, and said,

> Do you know what I have done to you? You call me Master and Lord, and you say well, for so I am. If then I, being your Lord and Master, have washed your feet, you also ought to wash one another's feet. For I have given you an example, that I have done to you, so you do also (John 13:12-15).

The Christian concept of existence can be summarized as follows: God is the Lord and the Omnipotent, and omnipotent is his sway. His omnipotent rule is love and "love in seriousness" — in such seriousness that this love, as the life of Jesus reveals, becomes his destiny.

This love — we must emphasize it again — indicates the ever incomprehensible decision of the Infinite that the finite should exist, should be itself, should flourish and reach perfection. God's love is his will that the person should exist in a state of dignity and freedom which may not be violated, which God himself respects and does not force even when it sets itself against his will.

This fundamental element of Christian existence shall again be realized in the church, and shall be made possible by the personal working of the Holy Spirit. It begins with the renouncing of force and constraint, and with the confidence that the apparent powerlessness which ensues will yet lead to good. It also demands a silent reverence even if the person appealed to closes his mind or rebels, even if his freedom says no when it should say yes. The final criterion for the history of the church is not the height of her cultural achievement, not even of her religious culture, but the degree of clarity with which her members, both clergy and laity, recognize that the vital powers which Christ has given the church become active only insofar as they take the form not of lordship but of love and service. This they must recognize, and act accordingly.

The transformation of authority into service and of power into love is one with the charge to preach the gospel. For the gospel means the revelation of the mystery that God has eternally willed that his omnipotence should be love, love in all seriousness; this will has been carried out in the creation, redemption and sanctification of men and of the world. But the history of the church is the history of the understanding of this task attained by her members, of the sincerity of their will to fulfill it, and of the measure in which this attempt succeeds. But since the church consists of human beings, this history is a concatenation of effort, advances and realizations. Between these lie periods of relapse when authority is understood as lordship and power as force.

We cannot apply the modern idea of progress to the history of the church. This idea constitutes a fatal illusion. The noblest thing that lives in man is the will to become better and ever better; it is a yearning for perfection. But this will and this yearning are personal. They can be realized only in freedom — with the attendant danger of the possibility of *yes* or *no,* of success and failure. The idea of progress confuses all this with the concept of "evolution," which is derived from the determinism of nature. This deceives man about the character of his existence and paralyzes his noblest powers. The realization of the charge given to the church is of another kind. It takes place — or does not — in trial, decision, steadfastness or failure.

Hence, the fundamental Christian concept of judgment refers also to the church — more exactly to the embodiment of the church in the individual cleric and layman. Much of the history of the church, her persecutions, her powerlessness and failure — "much" not "all," for we must not forget that the church also faces a resolute hostility — much of this is a judgment; that is, the consequence, or rather the penalty, for failing to carry out her great charge.

In our pluralistic age the repeated question, by what sign the church can be recognized as the church of the Lord, becomes particularly urgent. In view of the thoughts we have suggested the answer must be, "It can be recognized by the fact that it turns authority into service, and power into love." This is implied in the statement of Christ which St. John records in the last discourse: "By this shall all men know that you are my disciples, if you have love one for another" (13:35).

Of course the questioner must also consider that this answer cannot be read off like the indicator of a barometer. There are certain prerequisites for receiving it, especially the will to understand, and also to grant to the church what we always claim for ourselves — the recognition of the insufficiency of all things human. And the church is composed of human beings. . . .

Finally, we must indicate, though briefly, something which characterizes the living being which we call the church: namely, that it has a cosmic relation. This relation is essential to it even where its external measure is slight, for it is primarily and essentially of a qualitative rather than a quantitative nature, though it is quantitative also when regarded as a goal.

Instructed by Revelation, the church sees the world not as the modern concept of nature sees it, which, even while recognizing the cosmos fundamentally as finite, acts as if nature were infinite, or more precisely, absolute — the one and all, without beginning or end, the simple existent, which is its own cause and can be understood through itself alone. Rather, the church regards the world as a creation, a work, determined and supported by the one and only absolute, the Creator. From this point of view she considers the world, in its smallest details, as a whole.

Whether the church realizes this wholeness in her attitude — that means, gives to every creature the freedom of being and development which is its due according to the will of the Creator — is another question.

We must also add that this cosmic relation means something other than indefinite generality. The Catholicity which, from her very origin, is possible for the church and is the mission given to her, also implies unmistakable identity and clear recognizability.

The Church of the Lord, pages 36–43 (1965)

Christ Is the Church

Jesus knew that he and his message were absolutely decisive, so he wished this to be carried on "to all nations and even to the end of the world" (Matthew 28:19–20). But in his comments about this continuation of his message, the concept of a book does not occur. . . . He does speak repeatedly of the written word of God, but always in reference to the Old Testament. The means of propagating his own message would be the living proclamation by those whom he had chosen (Acts 1:2). The methods by which they would carry out their mission were left to them: the spoken and the written word, commemorative action, deeds that gave testimony, and exemplary living, a combination upon which the fullness of the Spirit was bestowed through the events of the day of Pentecost and which thereafter continued to the end of time. This combination is the church.

Christ guarantees the reality of the living Father; but the true image of Christ is guaranteed by the church, or, more precisely, by the Holy Spirit who speaks in her. Of her Jesus says, "He that hears you hears me; and he that despises you despises me; and he that despises me, despises him that sent me" (Luke 10:16). In the word of the church he is speaking; in his words the Father speaks.

The Scriptures are a living element of the church. They have sprung from her, completed in the course of the first century and gathered into a valid canon by the church herself around the turn of the century. It is the church of Christ who again and again exhorts the individual to give up his own soul in order to receive it again, renewed and restored to its true nature.

The exhortation is such that it cannot be pronounced by the autonomous will of the person addressed, but it springs from a reality which is independent of his pleasure. If he misunderstands the message, it corrects him. If he fabricates a Christ according to his own wishes, it defends the true image. If he eliminates from the figure of Christ the elements that scandalize him, it emphasizes these. In this constant encounter with the concrete, contemporary church, the figure of Christ constantly rises up again intact and unimpaired in its sovereignty, bearing witness to the Father as he truly is.

All this means that the step which really led to the freedom of faith in the complete reality of Christ, and through him in the sovereignty of the living God, is the belief that Christ speaks in the church, so that he who hears her hears Christ himself (Luke 10:16).

This statement may sound strange at a time when it has become for many a matter of course to hold that he who submits to the church loses the freedom of the gospel. In actual fact the church educates us for Christian freedom. Of course this freedom means something other than the psychological possibility of choosing what suits our taste or the philosophical autonomy to judge right and wrong according to our own standards. It means that the one who is ready to believe is constantly freed from the constraint of psychological, sociological, historical and other presumptions, and brought before the complete reality of the God who reveals himself in Christ.

The Church of the Lord, pages 63–64 (1965)

Chapter 6

We Are the Church

The People of God

There is one image which is today seemingly predominant in men's thoughts — the image of the people of God. It is marvelously vivid and full of movement, and expresses immediately something that is particularly important for the thought of our time: the historical element, the church's existing and working in time, her wandering and struggling. But we must not forget the other image which the Lord himself contributed to Christian thought when he spoke of the edifice that he would build upon the rock.

The church, as St. Paul explains, developing the words of his Master, is that great whole which grows and matures as a living being and sends forth various particular forms — branches of the vine. This grows throughout the course of history and shall fill the whole earth, indeed, shall go beyond the earth and transform the whole creation. But the church is also "where two or three are gathered together in the name of Jesus" and he is in their midst.

The church will ultimately be that precious adamantine structure, built of noble gems glistening in the brightness of eternal light (as the final chapters of the Apocalypse describe her). But she will also reveal the tender beauty of the bride going to meet her spouse. She will be both, passing from one image to the other. This is of her very nature, and is in effect even in our day. There is in her a constant activity and also an abiding sameness.

The church is so very much alive that she lives in every hour of history, determines it and receives from it material for growth. She is stirred to growth but also narrowed and hardened, questioned by each moment of history, and in answer unfolds what has lain hidden within her. But the church is also the unflinching one, guarding the yea and nay of the truth, so that scripture can make a very severe statement, that he who does not listen to her, knowing what he does, should be regarded "as a heathen and a public sinner."

All these images, which express real power, real responsibility and dignity, are again veiled by the mystery of the eschatological elements. They can be refuted at every point by the appearances of history. They must be believed, and their fulfillment must be hoped for and awaited. They express power and qualities of majesty and dignity which are already operative in every place, however insignificant, but must not be interpreted in terms of earthly and historical glory. Their embodiment in transforming glory is reserved for the future — the absolute future which lies beyond the return of the Lord.

The Church of the Lord, pages 112–114 (1965)

Christ Bound Himself

This is the very core of Christian thought, that the Son of God does not keep himself isolated from human reality by some metaphysical barrier, but has entered into this reality, and by this very fact has bound himself. If we have once noticed this situation we see that it began much earlier, by the very fact that God created the world. Have we ever thought about that — not just "thought," but deeply reflected, with mind and heart — what it means that God created the world? He, the infinite one, created our finite world. However immeasurably it may extend into the realm of cosmic vastness or microscopic minuteness, however inexhaustible in its forms and unfathomable in its nature, in comparison with God it is still something "small." But since God has created it, it exists, and nothing can alter that fact. Let us accept the thought: Since the creation of the world, God no longer exists without the world. Logically, that statement is nonsense, for the words "since" and "no longer" express the element of time and time only comes into being with the world. But we cannot speak in any other way, and the meaning of the statement is probably evident. It is something monstrous, something scandalous, unless we consider it with piety and obedience. But does this not indicate a "binding" of God, through his own sovereign will? This bond shall never be severed, since Revelation tells us that this world of ours, after its destruction, shall arise as a "new heaven and a new earth." Is it not a "binding" that God created man, who shall never be annihilated? Hence, there exists forever the sacred "I-Thou" relation between God and man into which man has been called by God, and in which the one who has been called can say, "My Lord and my God."

The tremendous and incomprehensible thing of which Revelation tells us and which, through faith, becomes the core of our existence, is just this sublime truth, that God has bound himself for our sake. Therefore it is not proper for man to presume to concern himself about God's freedom, but he should accept with adoration and love what grace bestows upon him.

Not classical humanism, not oriental profundity of thought, not the modern concept of the superman has ever regarded man and the world as seriously as has the Christian faith. They have never been as highly valued as in the Christian revelation. If we ask how God is disposed toward man, into what relation with himself God has admitted man, then we are told something which would be blasphemy if we asserted it on our own initiative. But, since God himself says it, we may adore it and call it love — for this is the love which St. John says originates not in man but in God (1 John 4:10). This is a mystery of magnanimity so great that it overwhelms us. Let us beware of trying to prescribe to God the Lord how he should be or what he should do. A god whom we conceive of according to our standards of what constitutes proper divinity would be a man-made image. The true God is as he revealed himself. And he reveals himself as the one who thinks and does those things which we have considered.

His sovereign freedom has also bound itself by the church. We must take care so that nothing false may creep into our thoughts about this church. Let us not say "God must be free," and mean thereby "I wish to be my own master." The fact that God has bound himself, which is basic for my Christian existence, means also that I myself am bound. If God wills that I should exist, then he binds himself in love to keep me always dependent upon him. And so it would be blasphemy if I declared that I did not wish to exist. Rather, I should render him the obedience of my existence and carry it out in the obedience of action. If God wills that the church should exist, in the plain sense of an unambiguous historicity, then he binds himself in love to realize his grace through her, and by that very fact I am bound to accept her as that which he wished her to be.

The Church of the Lord, pages 92–94 (1965)

Contemporaneity with Jesus Christ

In the sense of his immediate historical reality Jesus of Nazareth can never become my contemporary; but, his messengers can, and in them he himself "comes" (Luke 10:16). The sum total of his messengers is the church, and every age is contemporary with her for she goes on through all the ages. The teacher who speaks of Christ and his message; the priest who explains the word and baptizes; the celebration of the eucharist for which the congregation assembles around the altar; the bishop and the teachers of the faith, whom he ordains — all this is the church. Through her I receive the message. The church also includes the believing family in whose atmosphere I receive the spirit and the language of Christianity; the people of the congregation among whom I stand at the altar; the others everywhere in the world who know that they are one in the unity of faith. All these, living and teaching, are really and immediately my contemporaries. Their whole humanity, the good and also the questionable, joins in proclaiming the message and demands to be included and supported in the Christian "we."

In all of this Christ is present and speaks to me. He speaks to me not as an isolated figure, but as the church.

But in what a strange relation she stands to him who speaks in her! Everything in the church is so full of the human elements — commonplace, ordinary, even wicked human elements. How much has been perpetuated in theories, rules, regulations and prescriptions which did not belong to the original message! How many accretions have adhered to her in the long passage through history! What a great responsibility rests upon her for all that has been said and done, or left unsaid and neglected in her name!

So the question naturally arises: Is this the witness which I can and should believe? Is this the figure through which the Holy Spirit speaks — he who stepped into history on the day of Pentecost and shall "lead us into all truth," as Jesus promised (John 16:13)? The whole difficulty of what Kierkegaard called the "absolute paradox" rushes down upon us. But the way of faith leads through it, for hereby I find out about Christ. To think that one can have direct experience of him is an illusion, for even the book of the New Testament, which we might suppose would bring the reader immediately before Christ, really belongs to the church. The enormity of the problems which arise at this point is attested to by all that we call New Testament scholarship and also by those persons who say that they cannot find in these texts any morally binding word of God. And yet God is speaking here.

The step into the church is certainly not what a commonplace polemic thinks it to be: an escape into indolence, a surrender of one's own responsibility to priest, bishop or Pope. This may be true in individual cases, of course, just as the will to make one's own decision may be subjectivistic self-assertion. But the truth is that we learn about Jesus only through the church. But again and again we experience the effects of the all-too-human element in the church. Again and again we hear — not only from others but from our own feelings — the objection: what I meet here cannot be the church as Christ means her to be; and again and again we must decide: This is she; I believe!

Then we experience anew the reassuring, expanding and liberating effect that she produces, for the church is that which the polemic against her not only does not see but turns into its opposite. She is the guarantee, intended by Christ himself, that he can, out of the very freedom of his being, approach every man.

The Church of the Lord, pages 67 – 69 (1965)

Church, Personality and Community

What is the church? It is the kingdom of God in humanity. The kingdom of God — it is the epitome of Christianity. All that Christ was, all that he taught, did, created and suffered, is contained in these words. He has established the kingdom of God. The kingdom of God means that the Creator takes possession of his creature, penetrates it with his light; he fills its will and heart with his own burning love and the root of its being with his own divine peace, and he molds the entire spirit by the creative power which imposes a new form upon it. The kingdom of God means that God draws his creature to himself and makes it capable of receiving his own fullness; and that he bestows upon it the longing and the power to possess him. It means — alas, the words are so blunted by repetition and our hearts are so dull, or they would catch fire at the thought! — that the boundless fecundity of the divine Love seizes the creature and brings it to that second birth whereby it shares God's own nature and lives with a new life which springs from himself. In that rebirth the Father makes it his child in Christ Jesus through the Holy Ghost.

This union of the human being with God is God's kingdom. In it we belong to our Creator, and our Creator belongs to us.

Much more of profound significance could be said about this mystery, but we must be content with these few words.

This elevation of the creature is not a natural event but God's free act. It is bound up with the historical personality of Jesus of Nazareth and with the work which he accomplished at a particular period of history. Nor is it a natural process, but an operation of grace, exceeding all the forces of nature.

Let us examine it more closely. From the standpoint of God, it is something quite simple. But in the creature it develops to its maturity according to the forms and laws which God has established in the spirit of the human being.

God's kingdom resides in humanity. God takes possession of humanity as such, of the unity, welded by all the biological, geographical, cultural and social ties which bind one human being to others — that mysterious unity which, though composed entirely of individuals, is more than their sum. If this whole is to be taken hold of by God, it is not necessary that all people should be numerically included in it. It is sufficient that God's grace should take hold of the community, that something which transcends the individual. This, however, can be accomplished in a small representative group. The little flock at Pentecost was already humanity, because it was an objective community, of which the individual was a member; it was in a condition to expand, until it slowly included everything, as the mustard seed becomes the tree in which the birds of the air dwell. That is to say, we are concerned with a line of force, the direction along which the divine action operates. God takes possession of people, insofar as they reach out above their natural grasp; inasmuch as people belong to a supra-personal unity they are, or are capable of becoming, members of a community.

Therefore, as God's remodeling and uplifting power is directed toward the community, the church comes into being. The church is the kingdom in its supra-personal aspect — the human community, reborn into God's kingdom. The individual is the church, to the extent that the aim of that individual's life is to assist the building up of the community and he or she is a member, a cell of it. This, however, is the case insofar as that person is employing those capacities which have a more than merely individual reference and are ordained to the service of the whole; which work for it, give to it and receive from it. The church is the supra-personal, objective aspect of the kingdom of God — although, of course, it consists of individual persons.

The kingdom of God, however, has a subjective side as well: the individual soul, as God's grace takes possession of it in that private and unique individuality by which it exists for itself. The church embraces individuals as they reach out beyond themselves to others, capable and desirous of forming with them a community in which they themselves and the others are members. The individual personality, however, is also based upon itself, like a globe which revolves around its own axis; God's grace also takes possession of it. By this I do not mean that there exists in human beings a sphere which lies outside the church; that would be too superficial a notion. It is truer to say that the whole personality is in the church, with all that it is. Even in a person's most individual aspect, he or she is its member, although only insofar as this individuality and its powers are directed to the community. One's whole being belongs to it; it is in its social reference — each one's individuality related to its fellows and incorporated in the community. But the same individuality has an opposite pole; one's powers are also directed inward to build up a world in which that person is alone with himself or herself. In this aspect also an individual is the subject of God's grace.

God is the God of humanity as a whole. As such he is concerned with the supra-personal, the community; its members jointly find in him the social deity of which human society has need. But God is also the God of each individual; this is indeed the supreme and fullest revelation of his life — that for each individual he is "my God." God is the unique response to the unique need of every individual; possessed by each in the unique manner which that individual's unique personality requires; belonging to that person as to no other, in that person's unique nature. This is God's kingdom in the soul, the Christian personality.

Clearly this Christian personality is not a sphere lying outside the church, or something opposed to it; it is the church's organic opposite pole, demanded by its very nature, yet at the same time determined by it.

We have contrasted the kingdom of God as the church with the kingdom of God as personality. We were obliged to do so, in order to grasp clearly the distinctions between them. But the question arises, what is the relation between them?

We must reply at once and as emphatically as possible: They are not two things separable from each other, not two kingdoms. They are aspects of the same basic reality of the Christian life, the same fundamental mystery of grace. There is only one kingdom of

God, only one divine possession of the person by the Father, in Christ, through the Holy Ghost. But it develops along the two fundamental lines of all organic development, and it manifests itself in accordance with the two fundamental modes of human nature: in persons as they are self-contained and assert themselves as individuals, and in persons as they merge in the community which transcends their individuality.

The kingdom of God is at once the church and individual personality, and it is both *a priori* and of its very essence. It is definitely the church, for the church is the transfiguration of a person's nature by grace, so far as that person is within the community; and it is a kingdom of individual personality in every believer. It is thus both the church and the individual Christian. They are not independent spheres. Neither can be separated from the other, even if each one can be considered separately. On the contrary, of their nature and *a priori* they are interrelated and interdependent.

The nature of the community as Catholicism understands and realizes it is not such that individual personality has to struggle for self-preservation against it. It is not a power which violates personal individuality, as communism does, or any other variety of the totalitarian state. On the contrary, Catholic community presupposes from the outset and requires the free individual personalities as its components. In particular, the church is a community of beings who are not simply members and instruments of the whole, but are microcosms revolving on their own axes, that is, individual personalities. Mere individuals can constitute only herds or human anthills; community is a mutual relationship of personalities. This is an ethical requirement, for morality demands a free intercourse. It also results from the very structure of being, for it is only when units with their individual centers, their own *modus operandi* and a life of their own, come together that there can arise that unity — unique in its tension and flexibility, stable, yet rich in intrinsic possibilities of development — which is termed a community.

Christian personality is not so constituted that it is only as an afterthought associated with others to form a community; membership of the community does not originate in a concession made by one individual to another. It is not the case that individuals by nature independent of one another conclude a contract, by which each sacrifices a part of his or her independence, that by this concession each may save as much of it as possible. That is the view of society held by individualism. Personality, as Catholicism understands it, looks in every direction, and thus *a priori* and of its very nature is social, and an individual's entire being enters into society. A mere sum of individuals can produce only a crowd. If a large number join together merely by a contract for some definite object, the sole bond which constitutes their society will be this common purpose. A genuine community, on the contrary, cannot be formed in this way by individuals. It exists from the outset, and is a supra-individual reality, however hard it may be to comprehend from an intellectual conception of its nature.

It is this which fundamentally distinguishes the relationship between the community and the individual as Catholicism understands it from all one-sided conceptions of it, such as communism and the totalitarian state on the one hand, and individualism or even anarchy on the other. It is not based on a one-sided psychology or a mental construction, but on reality in its fullness. The Catholic's conception of personality differs from every type of individualism essentially, and not merely in degree. For the same individual who is a self-centered unit is at the same time conscious in his or her whole being that he or she is a member of the community, in this case the church. In the same way the community is not a mere feeble social restriction or state bondage, but something fundamentally different. It differs, as does a living being with its innumerable aspects, from an artificial construction without flesh and blood. The community realizes that it is made up of individuals, each one of whom constitutes a self-contained world and possesses a unique character. This is a fundamental truth which it is most important to understand thoroughly. Unless it is grasped, the Catholic view of the church, indeed of society, must be unintelligible. We must not get our sociological principles either from communism, state socialism, or individualism, for all these tear the living whole to pieces to exaggerate one portion of it. All are false and diseased. The Catholic conceptions of society and of individual personality start on the contrary — like all Catholic teaching — not from isolated axioms or one-sided psychological presuppositions, but from the integrity of real life apprehended without prejudice. By virtue of their nature men and women are both individual persons and members of a society. These two aspects of their being do not simply coexist; on the contrary, society exists already as a living seed in a person's individuality, and the latter in turn is necessarily presupposed by society as its foundation, though without prejudice to the relative independence of both these two primary forms of human life.

From this point of view also the Catholic type of humanity is reappearing at the present day, shaking off at last the spell of state worship on the one hand and of a disintegrating self-sufficiency on the other. Here, too, we are handling realities instead of words, and we recognize organic relationships instead of being dominated by abstract conceptions. It is for us to decide whether we shall allow ourselves to be re-enslaved, or remain conscious of our mission to be true to the fundamental nature of humanity and express it freely and faithfully in word and deed.

The church, then, is a society essentially bound up with individual personality, and the individual life of the Christian is of its very nature related to the community. Both together are required for the perfect realization of the kingdom of God. An electric current is impossible without its two poles; the one pole cannot exist, or even be conceived, without the other. In the same way the great fundamental Christian reality, the kingdom of God, is impossible, except as comprising both church and individual personality, each with its well-defined and distinctive nature, but essentially related to the other. There would be no church if its members were not at the same time mental microcosms, each self-subsistent and alone with God. There would be no Christian personality if it did not at the same time form part of the community as a living member. The soul elevated by grace is not something anterior to the church, as individuals originally isolated formed an alliance. Those who hold this view have failed completely to grasp the essence of Catholic personality. Nor does the church absorb the individual so that a man's or woman's personality can be realized only when they wrench themselves free from it. Those who think this do not know what the church is. When I affirm the church I am at the same time affirming individual personality, and when I speak of the interior life of the Christian, I imply the life of the Christian community.

Even now, however, the mutual relationship has not been fully stated. Both the church and the individual personality are necessary. Both, moreover, exist from the first; for neither can be traced back to the other. If anyone should attempt to ask which of the two is the more valuable in the sight of God, that person would see at once that it is a question which cannot be asked. For Christ died for the church, that he might make her, by his blood, a glorious church, not having spot or wrinkle. But he also died for every individual soul. The state, in its human weakness, sacrifices the individual to the society; God does not. The church and the individual personality — both, then, are equally primordial, equally essential, equally valuable. There is a profound difference, however, between these two expressions of the kingdom of God. Priority of rank belongs to the church. She has authority over the individual. Individual persons are subordinated to her: their will to hers, their judgment to hers and their interests to hers. The church is invested with the majesty of God and is the visible representative in face of the individual and the sum total of individuals. She possesses — within the limits imposed by her own nature and the nature of individual personality — the power which God possesses over the creature; she is authority. However aware individual personalities may be of their direct relation to God, and as God's children know that they are emancipated from tutors and governors, and although they enjoy personal communion with God, they are, notwithstanding, subject to the church as to God. "He that heareth you, heareth me." "Whatsoever thou shalt bind upon earth, shall be bound also in heaven." It is a profound paradox which, nevertheless, is in harmony with the nature of life and, as soon as the mind's eye is focused steadily upon it, self-evident.

The Church and the Individual

From all this one fact emerges. The personal life of the Christian is engaged to its profoundest depth in the church and is affected by her condition. Conversely, the church is to an incalculable degree affected by the spiritual condition of her members. What concerns the church concerns me. You see at once what this implies. It does not simply mean that a child, for instance, will be badly taught if the servant of the church who has charge of the child's education is inadequate to the task. On the contrary, between the individual and the church there is an organic solidarity of the most intimate kind. The same kingdom of God lives in the church and in the individual Catholic. The state of each is correlative, as the surface of the water is determined by the pipes which supply it. The individual can as little disassociate himself or herself from the state of the church — it would be the illusion of individualism — as the individual cell can disassociate itself from the state of health of the whole body. Conversely, it is a matter of incalculable concern for the church whether the faithful are men and women of strong and valuable personality and character. The church could never aim at a power, strength and depth to be achieved at the expense of the individual personalities of her members, for she would imperil the power, strength and depth of her own life. This must not be misunderstood. The church does not depend for her existence and essential nature upon the spiritual and moral condition of individuals; were this the case, she would not be an objective reality, and everything said hitherto has insisted upon her essential objectivity. In the concrete, the abundance and development of her life do depend in every age upon the extent to which her individual members have become what God intended them to be: developed personalities, each unique, with a unique vocation and unique capacities to be fulfilled. The relation between the church and the individual should never be understood as though either could develop at the expense of the other. This misconception is at the root of the un-Catholic attitude to this question. . . .

We are Catholic as far as we grasp — or rather, for this is insufficient — as far as we live the fact, indeed feel it as obvious in our very bones as something to be taken for granted, that the purity, greatness and strength of individual personality and of the church rise and fall together.

Tension between the Church and the Individual

You now realize, I am sure, how very far short of this Catholic frame of mind our ideas are, and even more our deepest and most immediate feelings — how far the contemporary tension between the community and the individual has affected our view of the relation between the church and the individual, thereby imperilling its very essence.

We are conscious of a tension between the church and the individual personality, and the most enthusiastic speeches cannot abolish it. It is not the tension of which we have already spoken, the tension inherent in the nature of their relationship, which is a source of health and life, but an unnatural and destructive tension. In the Middle Ages the objective reality of the church, like that of society in general, was directly experienced. The individual had been integrated into the social organism in which he or she freely developed a distinctive personality. At the Renaissance individuals attained a critical self-consciousness and asserted their own independence at the expense of the objective community. By so doing, however, they gradually lost sight of their profound dependence upon the entire social organism. Consequently, the modern person's consciousness of his or her own personality is no longer healthy, no longer bound up with the conscious life of the community. It has overshot the mark and detached itself from its organic context. Individuals cannot help feeling the church to be, with its claim to authority, a power hostile to themselves. No hatred pierces deeper than that between complementary forms of life, from which we may form some idea of what the tension involves.

It will be the mission of the coming age once more to envisage truly the relationship between the church and the individual. If this is to be achieved, our conceptions of society and individual personality must once more be adequate. Self-consciousness and the sense of organic life must again be brought into harmony, and the inherent interdependence of the church and the individual must again be accepted as a self-evident truth. Every age has its special task. This is equally true of the development of the religious life. To see how the church and the individual personality are mutually bound together, how they live the one by the other, and how, in this mutual relationship, we must seek the justification of ecclesiastical authority — to make this insight once more an integral part of our life and consciousness is the fundamental achievement to which our age is called.

If we wish to succeed in this task, we must free ourselves from the partial philosophies of the age, such as individualism, state socialism, or communism. Once more we must be wholeheartedly Catholic. Our thought and feeling must be determined by the essential nature of the Catholic position, must proceed from that direct insight into the center of reality which is the privilege of the genuine Catholic.

Individual personality starves in frigid isolation if it is cut off from the living community, and the church must necessarily be intolerable to those who fail to see in her the precondition of their most individual and personal life, who view her only as a power which confronts them and which, far from having any share in their most intimate, vital purpose, actually threatens or represses it. A person's living will cannot accept a church so conceived. Such a person must either rise in revolt against it, or else submit to it as the costly price of salvation. But the individual whose eyes have been opened to the meaning of the church experiences a great and liberating joy, for such individuals see that it is the living presupposition of their personal existence, the essential path to their perfection. They are aware of profound solidarity between their personal being and the church — how the one lives by the other, and how the life of the one is the strength of the other.

That we can love the church is at once the supreme grace which may be ours today, and the grace which we need most. Men and women of the present generation cannot love the church merely because they were born of Catholic parents; we are too conscious of our individual personalities. Just as little can that love be produced by the intoxication of oratory and mass meetings — it is not only in the sphere of civil life that such drugs have lost their efficacy. Nor can vague sentiments give us that love; our generation is too honest for that. One thing only can avail: a clear insight into the nature and significance of the church. We must realize that, as Christians, our personality is achieved in proportion as we are more closely incorporated into the church and as the church lives in us. When we address her, we say with deep understanding not "thou" but "I."

If I have really grasped these truths, I shall no longer regard the church as a spiritual police force, but blood of my own blood, the life of whose abundance I live. I shall see it as the all-embracing kingdom of my God, and his kingdom in my soul as its living counterpart. Then will the church be my mother and my queen, the bride of Christ. Then can I love her! And only then can I find peace!

We shall not be at peace with the church till we have reached the point at which we can love it. Not till then . . .

The Church and the Catholic, pages 33–47 (1922)

Part 4

Liturgy and Worship

Chapter 7

Congregation, Fellowship and Prayer

The Congregation and the Church

When churchgoers enter the sacred precincts they come as individuals, each with his particular talents and circumstances, worries and wishes. Each takes his own stand, confronting the others. Each is isolated from the others by all the sentiments summed up in the words "I – not you": indifference, strangeness, mistrust, superiority, dislike and enmity — by the hard crust developed in the struggle for existence and by the disappointments that past goodwill has experienced.

This, then, is the mental state of the average worshiper as he steps into church, stands or sits or kneels. Certainly there is as yet little of a *member of a congregation* about him. Leaving aside the questionable and the out-and-out wrong that this state brings with it — lovelessness, pride, ill will and so forth — let us try to get an idea of the kind of life that is pouring into the church. We have a roomful of people, each with his private thoughts, feelings, aims — a conglomeration of little separate worlds. The bearing of everyone present seems to say "I," or at best the "we" of his closest associations: his family, friends, dependents. But even this inclusion often really means little more than a widened self-esteem. The singular ego is stretched to a natural group-ego that is still far removed from genuine congregation. The true congregation is a gathering of those who belong to Christ, the holy people of God, united by faith and love.

Essentially it is of his making, a piece of new creation which finds expression in the bearing of its participants.

When we read the prayers of the Mass with this in mind, we notice that the word *I* appears very seldom, and never without a special reason. It is found quite clearly in the prayers at the foot of the altar, when each one present acknowledges his sins; and in the credo, when the individual, conscious of his personal responsibility, expresses his belief in divine revelation; in the prayers immediately preceding holy communion. (It is interesting that all these texts have been introduced in connection with some specific, often very minor event, and that they were not an original part of the Mass.) As a rule, *we* is used: *we* praise thee, *we* glorify thee, *we* adore thee; forgive *us,* help *us,* enlighten *us.* This *we* is not spontaneous, but the carefully nurtured fruit of genuine congregation.

Now we begin to see what we are after: not a communal experience; not the individual's great or joyous or overwhelming foretaste of the union of many before God which may sometime sweep through him, filling and sustaining him. Like all true experience, that is a gift of the hour which is given or withheld; it cannot be merited. Here, though, it is a question not of an experience, but of an accomplishment; not of a gift, but of a required deed.

If we are to get anywhere with these considerations, we must see how deeply immersed in self we are and — for all our talk of community — what thorough egoists. When we speak of community we seldom mean more than the experience of self-extension. Lifted up and out of our personal narrowness by the total vitality around us we feel suddenly stronger or more enthusiastic than otherwise. In reality, no matter how long and how often people are together, they always remain alone.

The real antonym of community is not the individual and his individualism, but the egoist and his selfishness. It is this that must first be overcome, and not by frequent and prolonged association, but by mastering the mind and will; this alone allows us to see others as they really are, to acknowledge and accept them, to make their desires and anxieties our own, to restrain ourselves for their sakes.

To do this we must have solitude, for only in solitude do we have a chance to see ourselves objectively and to free ourselves from our own chains. Someday, perhaps on some special occasion, we will realize what walls of indifference, disregard, enmity loom between us and the other man, and before Mass or during the introit we will make a real effort to break through them. We will remind ourselves that together we face God; together we are congregation — not only I and others in general, but this man, that woman over there and the believer next to me. In God's sight they are all as important as I am — perhaps much more so — braver, less selfish, nobler, more loving and fervent. Among these people whom I know only by their features, by their gestures, are perhaps great and holy souls with whom I am fortunate to find myself associated, because the surge of their prayers sweeps me along with it to God!

Then we will let the other believers into the inner circle of our lives, present ourselves to God with them, linking our intentions to theirs. We will consciously, earnestly pray the we of the liturgy, for from such things congregation is formed.

Until now we have spoken of congregation as the Christian "we" in its encounter with God, the community of those united by the same faith and by mutual love. But this is not all. The conception must include also those outside any particular building, even outside the church, for congregation reaches far beyond.

It is no closed circle, no organization or union with its own center. Each congregation is part of a whole that far surpasses any Sunday gathering; it embraces everyone who believes in Christ in the same city, the same country, over the whole earth. The congregation gathered in any one church is influenced by its particular circumstances, by its services, by the quality of its members and by the particular feasts that they are celebrating. It is a unit, but one that remains open; all who are bound to Christ are included in it.

Its center is the altar — every altar in every church — the altar that is simultaneously the center of the world. At Christ's table all the faithful are remembered, and all belong to the we that is spoken there.

Still we have not touched bottom. In the confiteor priest and faithful confess their sins. Their confession is addressed primarily to God, and in his presence alternately to each other, but it is also addressed to Mary, the mother of the Lord; to the archangel Michael; to John the Baptist and the apostles Peter and Paul; and to all the saints. Behind the archangel, who appears here as the leader of the heavenly hosts, stands the world of angels; and "the saints" means not only the great historical figures of sanctity which the word usually suggests, but all the saved, all who have gone home to God. In other parts of the Mass as well, those who already participate in eternal life are invoked, whereas in the memento for the dead after the consecration all those still in need of purification and prayer are remembered.

In other words, congregation stretches not only over the whole earth but also far beyond the borders of death. About those gathered around the altar, the horizons of time and space roll back, revealing as the real, sustaining community the whole of saved humanity.

This congregation *in toto* then is the church, sustainer of the holy act of worship. That the Mass is something quite different from the private religious act of an individual is obvious, but it is also more than the divine service of a group of individuals united by like beliefs (that of a sect, for instance). It is the church with all the breadth that the word implies, the universal church. We begin to visualize her scope when we read what Saints Paul and John write of her. There, even her ultimate earthly limits dissolve to make her one with all saved creation. Her attributes are "the new man," "the new heaven," and "the new earth" (Ephesians 2:16, 4:24; Revelation 21:1).

Nor is the church merely the sum total of the saved plus the totality of things; rather, it is a living unit, an organism formed and composed around a reigning, all-permeating figure: the spiritual Christ. She has full powers to proclaim Christ's teaching and bestow his sacraments; respect or disrespect to her involves God himself. What sustains the Mass is not only an endless legion of hearts and spirits, the faith and love of all creation, but also a supernatural society endowed with authority and bearing responsibilities.

Our task is to find our place in the enormous whole. This is not easy. Man has a tendency to spiritual intimacy and exclusiveness. There is also the resistance of modern religious feeling to the visible church in its realistic sense, resistance to office and order, to authority and constitutionality. We are all too subjective, inclined to count as truly religious only the direct and spontaneous experience; order and authority leave us cold. Here self-discipline is especially necessary. The text of the Mass repeatedly reveals that attitude which has been called *Roman,* an attitude that rests precisely upon the consciousness of formal institutional unity, God-given authority, law and order. This may strike us as strange, perhaps even as unreligious. . . . Not only are we as Christians "congregation," not only "saved mankind" and "new creation"; we ourselves are "church," so we must consent and patiently educate ourselves to this given role.

Meditations Before Mass, pages 99–104 (1939)

The Fellowship of the Liturgy

The liturgy does not say "I," but "we," unless the particular action which is being performed specifically requires the singular number (e.g., a personal declaration, certain prayers offered by the bishop or the priest in his official capacity, and so on). The liturgy is not celebrated by the individual, but by the body of the faithful. This is not composed merely of the persons who may be present in church; it is not just the assembled congregation. On the contrary, it reaches out beyond the bounds of space to embrace all the faithful on earth. Simultaneously, it reaches beyond the bounds of time to this extent: that the body which is praying on earth knows itself to be at one with those for whom time no longer exists, who, being perfected, exist in eternity.

Yet this definition does not exhaust the conception of the universality and all-embracingness which characterizes the fellowship of the liturgy. The entity that performs the liturgical actions is not merely the sum of all individual Catholics. It does consist of all these united in one body, but only insofar as this unity is of itself something apart from the millions which compose it. That something is the church. . . .

The church is self-contained, a structure-system of intricate and invisible vital principles; of means and ends; of activity and production; of people, organizations and laws. It does consist of the faithful, then; but it is more than the mere body of these, passively held together by a system of similar convictions and regulations. The faithful are actively united by a vital and fundamental principle common to them all. That principle is Christ himself; his life is ours, we are incorporated in him, we are his body, *Corpus Christi Mysticum* (cf. Romans 12:4 ff.; 1 Corinthians 12:4 ff.; Ephesians 1–4; Colossians 1:15 ff.; and elsewhere). The active force which governs this living unity, grafting each individual on to it, granting them a share in its fellowship and preserving this right for them, is the Holy Ghost (cf. 1 Corinthians 12:4 ff.). Every individual Catholic is a cell of this living organism or a member of this Body.

Each faithful individual is made aware of the unity which comprehends them on many and various occasions, but chiefly in the liturgy. In it they see themselves face to face with God, not as an entity, but as members of this unity. It is the unity which addresses God; the individual merely speaks in it, and it requires of the individual man or woman that they should know that they are a member of it.

It is on the plane of liturgical relations that the individual experiences the meaning of religious fellowship. The individual man and woman — provided that they actually desire to take part in the celebration of the liturgy — must realize that it is as members of the church that they, and the church within them, act and pray; they must know that in this higher unity they are at one with the rest of the faithful, and they must desire to be so. . . .

It is, furthermore, the task of the individual to apprehend clearly the ideal world of the liturgy. Individuals must shake off the narrow trammels of their own thoughts, and make a far more comprehensive world of ideas their own: they must go beyond their little personal aims and adopt the educative purpose of the great fellowship of the liturgy. It goes without saying, therefore, that they are obliged to take part in exercises which do not respond to the particular need of which they are conscious; that they must ask for things which do not directly concern them; they must espouse and plead before God causes which do not affect them personally, and which merely arise out of the needs of the community at large; they must at times — and this is inevitable in so richly developed a system of symbols, prayer and action — take part in proceedings of which they do not entirely, if at all, understand the significance.

All this is particularly difficult for modern people, who find it so hard to renounce their independence. And yet people who are perfectly ready to play a subordinate part in state and commercial affairs are all the more susceptible, and the more passionately reluctant to regulate their spiritual lives by dictates other than those of their private and personal requirements. The requirements of the liturgy can be summed up in one word — humility: humility by renunciation; that is to say, by the abdication of self-rule and self-sufficiency, and humility by positive action; that is to say, by the acceptance of the spiritual principles which the liturgy offers and which far transcend the little world of individual spiritual existence.

The demands of the liturgy's communal life wear a different aspect for the people who are less affected by its concrete and impersonal side. For the latter, the problem of fellowship does not so much consist in the question of how they are to assimilate the universal and, as it were, concrete element, at the same time subordinating themselves to and dovetailing into it. The difficulty rather lies in their being required to divide their existence with other people, to share the intimacy of their inner life, their feeling and willing, with others, and to know that they are united with these others in a higher unity. By others we do not mean one or two neighbors or a small circle of people congenial by reason of similar aims or special relations, but with all, even with those who are indifferent, adverse or even hostile.

The demand here resolves itself into the breaking down of the barriers which the more sensitive soul sets around its spiritual life. The soul must issue forth from these if it is to go among others and share their existence. Just as in the first case the community was perceived as a great concrete order, in the second it is perceived as a broad tissue of personal affairs, an endless interweaving of living, reciprocal relations. The sacrifice required in the first place is that of renouncing the right of self-determination in spiritual activity and in the second, that of renouncing spiritual isolation. There it is a question of subordinating self to a fixed and objective order, here of sharing life in common with other people. There humility is required, here charity and vigorous expansion of self. There the given spiritual content of the liturgy must be assimilated; here life must be lived in common with the other members of Christ's Body, their petitions included with one's own, their needs voiced as one's own. There "we" is the expression of selfless objectivity; here it signifies that the individuals who employ it are expanding their inner lives in order to include those of others, and to assimilate theirs to themselves. In the first case, the pride which insists upon independence and the aggressive intolerance often bred by individual existence must be overcome, while the entire system of communal aims and ideas must be assimilated. In the second, the repulsion occasioned by the strangeness of corporate life and the shrinking from self-expansion must be mastered, and exclusiveness triumphed over which leads us to desire only the company of such as we have ourselves chosen and to whom we have voluntarily opened out. Here, too, is required continual spiritual abnegation, a continuous projection of self at the desire of others, and a great and wonderful love which is ready to participate in another's life and to make that life its own.

Yet the subordination of self is actually facilitated by a peculiarity inherent in liturgical life itself. It forms at once the complement of and contrast to what has already been discussed. Let us call the disposition manifesting itself in the two forms indicated above the individualistic. Facing it stands the social disposition, which eagerly and consistently craves fellowship, and lives in terms of "we" just as involuntarily as the former bases itself on the exclusive "I." The social disposition will, when it is spiritually active, automatically seek out congenial associates; their joint striving toward union will be characterized by a firmness and decision alien to the liturgy. It is sufficient to recall in this connection the systems of spiritual association and fellowship peculiar to certain sects. Here at times the bounds of personality diminish to such an extent that all spiritual reserve is lost, and frequently all external reserve as well. Naturally this description only applies to extreme cases, but it still shows the tendency of the social urge in such dispositions. For this reason people like this will not find all their expectations immediately fulfilled in the liturgy. The fellowship of the liturgy will to them appear frigid and restricted; it follows that this fellowship, however complete and genuine it might be, still acts as a check upon unconditional self-surrender. The social urge is opposed by an equally powerful tendency which sees to it that a certain fixed boundary is maintained. The individual man and woman are, it is true, members of the whole — but they are only members. They are not utterly merged with it; they are added to it, but in such a way that they throughout remain entities, existing of themselves. This is notably borne out by the fact that the union of the members is not directly accomplished from individual to individual. It is accomplished by and in their joint aim, goal and spiritual resting place — God — by their identical creed, sacrifice and sacraments. In the liturgy it is of very rare occurrence that speech and response, action or gesture are immediately directed from one member of the fellowship to the other. (This does not apply, of course, to the communication between the hierarchical persons and the faithful. This relation is continual and direct.) When this does occur, it is generally worthwhile to observe the great restraint which characterizes such communication. It is governed by strict regulations. The individual is never drawn into contacts which are too extensively direct. Such members are always free to decide how far they are to get in touch, from the spiritual point of view, with others in that which is common to them all — in God. Take the kiss of peace, for instance; when it is performed according to the rubric it is a masterly manifestation of restrained and elevated social solidarity.

This is of great importance. It is hardly necessary to point out what would be the infallible consequences of attempting to transmit the consciousness of their fellowship in the liturgy directly from one individual to the other. The history of the sects teems with examples bearing on this point. For this reason the liturgy sets strict bounds between individuals. Their union is moderated by a continually watchful sentiment of disparity and by reciprocal reverence. Their fellowship notwithstanding, the one individual can never force his or her way into the intimacy of the other, never influence the latter's prayers and actions, never force upon the latter his or her own characteristics, feelings and perceptions. Their fellowship consists in community of intention, thought and language, in the direction of eyes and heart to the one aim; in their identical belief, the identical sacrifice which they offer, the divine food which nourishes them all alike; in the one God and Lord who unites them mystically in himself. But individuals in their quality of distinct corporeal entities do not themselves intrude upon each other's inner life.

It is this reserve alone which in the end makes fellowship in the liturgy possible; but for it the latter would be unendurable. By this reserve again the liturgy keeps all vulgarizing elements at a distance. It never allows the soul to feel that it is imprisoned with others, or that its independence and intimacy are threatened with invasion.

From the person of individualistic disposition, then, a sacrifice for the good of the community is required; from the person of social disposition, submission to the austere restraint which characterizes liturgical fellowship. While the former must accustom themselves to frequenting the company of their fellow members and must acknowledge that they are only a person among persons, the latter must learn to subscribe to the noble, restrained forms which etiquette requires in the house and at the court of the divine majesty.

The Spirit of the Liturgy, pages 141–149 (1918)

The Prayer of the Liturgy

The primary and exclusive aim of the liturgy is not the expression of the individual's reverence and worship for God. It is not even concerned with the awakening, formation and sanctification of the individual soul as such. Nor does the onus of liturgical action and prayer rest with the individual; it does not even rest with the collective groups, composed of numerous individuals, who periodically achieve a limited and intermittent unity in their capacity as the congregation of the church. The liturgical entity consists rather of the united body of the faithful — the church — a body which infinitely outnumbers the mere congregation. The liturgy is the church's public and lawful act of worship and it is performed and conducted by the officials whom the church herself has designated for the post — her priests. In the liturgy God is to be honored by the body of the faithful, and the faithful are to derive sanctification from this act of worship. It is important that this objective nature of the liturgy should be fully understood. . . . The fact that the individual Catholic, by his or her absorption into the higher unity, finds unity, finds liberty and discipline, originates in the twofold nature of the human being, who is both social and solitary. . . .

    The prayers of the liturgy are entirely governed by and interwoven with dogma. Those who are unfamiliar with liturgical prayers often regard them as theological formulae, artistic and didactic, until on closer acquaintance they suddenly perceive and admit that the clear-cut, lucidly constructed phrases are full of interior enlightenment. To give an outstanding example, the wonderful collects of the Masses of Sunday may be quoted. Wherever the stream of prayer wells abundantly upward, it is always guided into safe channels by means of plain and lucid thought. Interspersed among the pages of the missal and the breviary are readings from Holy Scripture and from the works of the fathers, which continually stimulate thought. Often these readings are introduced and concluded by short prayers of a characteristically contemplative and reflective nature — the antiphons — during which what has been heard or read has time to cease echoing and to sink into the mind. The liturgy, the *lex orandi,* is, according to the old proverb, the law of faith, the *lex credendi,* as well. It is the treasure house of the thought of Revelation. . . .

    In any form of prayer, therefore, which is intended for the ultimate use of a corporate body, the whole fullness of religious truth must be included.

    Here, too, the liturgy is our teacher. It condenses into prayer the entire body of religious truth. Indeed, it is nothing else but truth expressed in terms of prayer. It is the great fundamental truths which above all fill the liturgy: God in his mighty reality, perfection and greatness, One, and Three in One; his creation, providence and omnipresence; sin, justification and the desire of salvation; the

Redeemer and his kingdom; the four last things [death, purgatory, heaven and hell]. Such an overwhelming abundance of truth can never pall, but continues to be, day after day, all things to all people, ever fresh and inexhaustible. . . .

The liturgy as a whole is not favorable to exuberance of feeling. Emotion glows in its depths, but it merely smolders, like the fiery heart of the volcano whose summit stands out clear and serene against the quiet sky. The liturgy is emotion, but it is emotion under the strictest control. We are made particularly aware of this at holy Mass, and it applies equally to the prayers of the ordinary and of the canon, and to those of the proper of the time. Among them are to be found masterpieces of spiritual restraint.

The restraint characteristic of the liturgy is at times very pronounced, making this form of prayer appear at first as a frigid intellectual production, until we gradually grow familiar with it and realize what vitality pulsates in the clear, measured forms. . . .

If prayer is ultimately to be fruitful and beneficial to a corporate body it must be intense and profound, but at the same time normal in tone. The wonderful verses of the hymn (from the Benedictine breviary, Tuesday Lauds, the prayer of daybreak) — hardly translatable, so full are they of penetrating insight — may be quoted in this connection:

Laeti bibamus sobriam
Ebrietatem Spiritus . . .

(Let us joyfully taste
of the sober drunkenness of the Spirit . . .)

Certainly we must not try to measure off the lawful share of emotion with a foot-rule; but where a plain and straightforward expression suffices we must neither aggrandize nor embellish it. A simple method of speech is always preferred to an overloaded one. . . .

Then the liturgy is wonderfully reserved. It scarcely even expresses certain aspects of spiritual surrender and submission, or else it veils them in such rich imagery that the soul still feels that it is hidden and secure. The prayer of the church does not probe and lay bare the heart's secrets; it is as restrained in thought as in imagery. It does, it is true, awaken very profound and very tender emotions and impulses, but it leaves them hidden. There are certain feelings of surrender, certain aspects of interior candor, which cannot be publicly proclaimed, at any rate in the entirety, without danger to spiritual modesty. The liturgy has perfected a masterly instrument which has made it possible for us to express our inner life in all its fullness and depth, without divulging our secrets — *secretum meum mihi.* We can pour out our hearts and still feel that nothing has been dragged to light that should remain hidden. . . .

Attention has already been called to the deep and fruitful emotion which is contained in the liturgy. It also embraces the two fundamental forces of human existence: nature and civilization.

In the liturgy the voice of nature makes itself heard clearly and decisively. We only need to read the psalms to see humanity as it really is. There the soul is shown as courageous and despondent, happy and sorrowful; full of noble intentions, but of sin and struggles as well, zealous for everything that is good; and then again apathetic and dejected. Or let us take the readings from the Old Testament. How frankly human nature is revealed in them! The same thing applies to the church's words of ordination and to the prayers used in administering the sacraments. A truly refreshing spontaneity characterizes them; they call things by their names. Humans are full of weakness and error, and the liturgy acknowledges this. Human nature is inexplicable, a tangled web of splendor and misery, of greatness and baseness, and as such it appears in the prayer of the church. Here we find no carefully adapted portrait from which the harsh and unpleasing traits have been excluded, but humanity as it is.

Not less rich is the liturgy's cultural heritage. We become conscious of the fact that many centuries have cooperated in its formation and have bequeathed to it their best. They have fashioned its language; expanded its ideas and conceptions in every direction; developed its beauty and construction down to the smallest detail — the short verses and finely-forged links of the prayers, the artistic form of the Divine Office and of the Mass, and the wonderful whole that is the ecclesiastical year. Action, narrative and choral forms combine to produce the cumulative effect. The style of the individual forms continually varies — simple and clear in the Hours, rich in mystery on the festivals of Mary, resplendent on the more modern feasts, delightful and full of charm in the offices of the early virgin martyrs. To this we should add the entire group of ritual gestures and action, the liturgical vessels and vestments, and the works of sculptors and artists and musicians.

In all this is an important lesson on liturgical practice. Religion needs civilization. By civilization we mean the essence of the most valuable products of people's creative, constructive and organizing powers — works of art, science, social order and the like. In the liturgy it is civilization's task to give durable form and expression to the treasure of truths, aims and supernatural activity which God has delivered to us by revelation, to distill its quintessence, and to relate this to life in all its multiplicity. Civilization is incapable of creating a religion, but it can supply the latter with a *modus operandi* so that it can freely engage in its beneficent activity. That is the real meaning of the old proverb, *philosophia ancilla theologiae* — philosophy is the handmaid of theology. It applies to all the products of civilization, and the church has always acted in accordance with it. Thus she knew very well what she was doing, for instance, when she absolutely obliged the Order of Saint Francis — brimming over with high aspiration and spiritual energy and initiative — to adopt a certain standard of living, property, learning and so on. Only a prejudiced mind with no conception of the fundamental conditions essential to normal spiritual life would see in this any deterioration of the first high aims. By her action in the matter the church, on the contrary, prepared the ground for the Order, so that in the end it could remain healthy and productive. Individuals, or short waves of enthusiasm, can to a wide degree dispense with learning and culture. This is proved by the beginnings of the desert orders in Egypt, and of the mendicant friars and by holy people in all ages. But, generally speaking, a fairly high degree of genuine learning and culture is necessary in the long run, in order to keep spiritual life healthy. By means of these two things spiritual life retains its energy, clarity and catholicity. Culture preserves spiritual life from the unhealthy, eccentric and one-sided elements with which it tends to get involved only too easily. Culture enables religion to express itself, and helps it to distinguish what is essential from what is non-essential — the means from the end and the path from the goal. The church has always condemned every attempt at attacking science, art, property and so on. The same church which so resolutely stresses the "one thing necessary," and which upholds with the greatest impressiveness the teaching of the evangelical counsels — that we must be ready to sacrifice everything for the sake of eternal salvation — nevertheless desires, as a rule, that spiritual life should be impregnated with the wholesome salt of genuine and lofty culture.

But spiritual life is in precisely as great a need of the subsoil of healthy nature — "grace takes nature for granted." The church has clearly shown her views on the subject by the gigantic struggles waged against Gnosticism and Manichaeism, against Catharists and the Albigenses, against Jansenism and every kind of fanaticism. This was done by the same church which, in the face of Pelagius and Celestius, of Jovinian and Helvidius, and of the immoderate exaltation of nature, powerfully confirmed the existence of grace and of the supernatural order and asserted that the Christian must overcome nature. The lack of fruitful and lofty culture causes spiritual life to grow numbed and narrow; the lack of the subsoil of healthy nature makes it develop on mawkish, perverted and unfruitful lines. If the cultural element of prayer declines, the ideas become impoverished, the language coarse, the imagery clumsy and monotonous; in the same way, when the lifeblood of nature no longer flows vigorously in its veins, the ideas become empty and tedious, the emotion paltry and artificial and the imagery lifeless and insipid. Both — the lack of natural vigor and the lack of lofty culture — together constitute what we call barbarism, i.e., the exact contradiction of that *scientia vocis* which is revealed in liturgical prayer and is reverenced by the liturgy itself as the sublime prerogative of the holy Creative Principle.

(The above remarks must not be misunderstood. Certainly the grace of God is self-sufficient; neither nature nor the work of a person is necessary in order that a soul may be sanctified. God can awaken of these stones children to Abraham. But as a rule he wishes that everything belonging to a person in the way of good, lofty, natural and cultural possessions shall be placed at the disposal of religion and so to serve the kingdom of God. He has interconnected the natural and the supernatural orders, and has given natural things a place in the scheme of his supernatural designs. It is the duty of his representatives on earth, ecclesiastical authority, to decide how and to what extent these natural means of attaining the supernatural goal are to be utilized.)

Prayer must be simple, wholesome and powerful. It must be closely related to actuality and not afraid to call things by their names. In prayer we must find our entire life over again. On the other hand, prayer must be rich in ideas and powerful images and speak a developed but restrained language; its construction must be clear and obvious to the simple person, stimulating and refreshing to the person of culture. It must be intimately blended with an erudition which is in nowise obtrusive, but which is rooted in breadth of spiritual outlook and in inward restraint of thought, volition and emotion.

That is precisely the way in which the prayer of the liturgy has been formed.

The Spirit of the Liturgy, pages 121–122; 124; 127; 129; 130–132; 136–140 (1918)

Chapter 8

Liturgy: Playful and Serious

The Playfulness of the Liturgy

The church . . . embraces a sphere which is in a special sense free from purpose. That is the liturgy. The latter certainly comprehends a whole system of aims and purposes, as well as the instruments to accomplish them. It is the business of the sacraments to act as the channels of certain graces. This mediation is easily and quickly accomplished when the necessary conditions are present. The administration of the sacraments is an example of a liturgical action which is strictly confined to the one object. Of course, it can be said of the liturgy, as of every action and every prayer which it contains, that it is directed toward the providing of spiritual instruction. This is perfectly true. But the liturgy has no thought-out, deliberate, detailed plan of instruction. In order to sense the difference it is sufficient to compare a week of the ecclesiastical year with the spiritual exercises of Saint Ignatius. In the latter every element is determined by deliberate choice and everything is directed toward the production of a certain spiritual and didactic result; each exercise, each prayer, even the way in which the hours of repose are passed, all aim at one thing: the conversion of the will. It is not so with the liturgy. The fact that it has no place in the spiritual exercises is a proof of this. The liturgy wishes to teach, but not by means of an artificial system of aim-conscious educational influences; it simply creates an entire spiritual world in which the soul can live according to the requirements of its nature. The difference resembles that which exists between a gymnasium, in which every detail of the apparatus and every exercise aims at a calculated effect, and the open woods and fields. In the first everything is consciously directed toward discipline and development; in the second life is lived with nature, and internal growth takes place in her. The liturgy creates a universe brimming with fruitful spiritual life and allows the soul to wander about in it at will and to develop itself there. The abundance of prayers, ideas and actions, and the whole arrangement of the calendar are incomprehensible when they are measured by the objective standard of suitability for a purpose. The liturgy has no purpose or, at least, it cannot be considered from the standpoint of purpose. It is not a means which is adapted to attain a certain end — it is an end in itself. This fact is important: If we overlook it, we labor to find all kinds of didactic purposes in the liturgy which may certainly be stowed away somewhere but are not actually evident.

When the liturgy is rightly regarded, it cannot be said to have a purpose, because it does not exist for the sake of humanity, but for the sake of God. In the liturgy we are no longer concerned with ourselves; our gaze is directed toward God. In it we are not so much intended to edify ourselves as to contemplate God's majesty. The liturgy means that the soul exists in God's presence, originates in him, lives in a world of divine realities, truths, mysteries and symbols, and really lives its true, characteristic and fruitful life. (The fact that the liturgy moralizes so little is consistent with this conception. In the liturgy the soul forms itself, not by means of deliberate teaching and the exercise of virtue, but by the fact that it exists in the light of eternal truth and is naturally and supernaturally robust.)

There are two very profound passages in Holy Scripture which are quite decisive on the point. One is found in the description of Ezekiel's vision (Ezekiel 1:4 ff., especially 12, 17, 20, 24, and 10:9 ff.). Let us consider the flaming cherubim, who "every one of them went straight forward, whither the impulse of the Spirit was to go . . . and they turned not when they went . . . ran and returned like flashes of lightning . . . went . . . and stood . . . and were lifted up from the earth . . . the noise of their wings was like the noise of many waters . . . and when they stood, their wings were let down." How aimless they are! How discouraging for the zealous partisans of reasonable suitability for a purpose! They are only pure motion, powerful and splendid, acting according to the direction of the Spirit, desiring nothing save to express its inner drift and its interior glow and force. They are the living image of the liturgy.

In the second passage it is eternal Wisdom which speaks: "I was with him, forming all things, and was delighted every day, playing before him at all times, playing in the world . . ." (Proverbs 8:30, 31).

This is conclusive. It is the delight of the eternal Father that Wisdom (the Son, the perfect fullness of truth) should pour out its eternal essence before him in all its ineffable splendor, without any purpose — for what purpose should it have? — but full of decisive meaning, in pure and vocal happiness; the Son plays before the Father.

Such is the life of the highest beings, the angels, who, without a purpose and as the Spirit stirs them, move before God and are a mystic diversion and a living song before him.

In the earthly sphere there are two phenomena which tend in the same direction: the play of the child and the creation of the artist.

The child, when it plays, does not aim at anything. It has no purpose. It does not want to do anything but exercise its youthful powers, pour forth its life in an aimless series of movements, words and actions, and by this to develop and realize itself more fully; all of this is purposeless, but full of meaning nevertheless, the significance lying in the unchecked revelation of this youthful life in thoughts and words and movements and actions, in the capture and expression of its nature and in the fact of its existence. And because it does not aim at anything in particular, because it streams unbroken and spontaneously forth, its utterance will be harmonious, its form clear and fine; its expression will of itself become picture and dance, rhyme, melody and song. That is what play means; it is life, pouring itself forth without an aim, seizing upon riches from its own abundant store, significant through the fact of its existence. It will be beautiful, too, if it is left to itself, and if no futile advice and pedagogic attempts at enlightenment foist upon it a host of aims and purposes, thus denaturing it.

As life progresses, conflicts ensue, and it appears to grow ugly and discordant. Human beings set before themselves what they want to do and what they should do, and try to realize this in their lives. In the course of these endeavors they learn that many obstacles stand in their way, and they perceive that it is very seldom that they can attain their ideal.

It is in a different order, in the imaginary sphere of representation, that people try to reconcile the contradiction between that which they wish to be and that which they are. In art they try to harmonize the ideal and the actual, that which they ought to be and that which they are, the soul within and nature without, the body and the soul. Such are the visions of art. It has no didactic aims; it is not intended to inculcate certain truths and virtues. A true artist has never had such an end in view. In art, he or she desires to do nothing but overcome the discord to which we have referred and express in the sphere of representation the higher life of which he or she stands in need—which, in actuality, any artist has only approximately attained. Artists merely want to give life to their being and its longing, to give external form to the inner truth. People who contemplate a work of art should not expect anything of it, but they should be able to linger before it, moving freely, becoming conscious of their own better nature and sensing the fulfillment of their most intimate longings. They should not reason and chop logic, or look for instruction and good advice from it.

The liturgy offers something higher. In it people, with the aid of grace, are given the opportunity of realizing their fundamental essence, of really becoming that which according to their divine destiny they should be and long to be: children of God. In the liturgy a person is to go unto God, who gives joy to youth. All this is, of course, on the supernatural plane, but it corresponds to the same degree to the inner needs of a person's nature. Because the life of the liturgy is higher than that to which customary reality gives both the opportunity and form of expression, it adopts suitable forms and methods from that sphere in which alone they are to be found, that is to say, from art. It speaks measuredly and melodiously; it employs formal, rhythmic gestures; it is clothed in colors and garments foreign to everyday life; it is carried out in places and at hours which have been co-ordinated and systematized according to more sublime laws than ours. It is in the highest sense the life of a child, in which everything is picture, melody and song.

Such is the wonderful fact which the liturgy demonstrates; it unites art and reality in a supernatural childhood before God. That which formerly existed in the world of unreality only, and was rendered in art as the expression of mature human life, has here become reality. These forms are the vital expression of real and frankly supernatural life. But this has one thing in common with the play of the child and the life of art — it has no purpose, but it is full of profound meaning. It is not work, but play. To be at play, or to fashion a work of art in God's sight — not to create, but to exist — such is the essence of the liturgy. From this is derived its sublime mingling of profound earnestness and divine joyfulness. The fact that the liturgy gives a thousand strict and careful directions on the quality of the language, gestures, colors, garments and instruments which it employs can only be understood by those who are able to take art and play seriously. Have you ever noticed how gravely children draw up the rules of their games — on the form of the melody, the position of the hands, the meaning of this stick and that tree? It is for the sake of the silly people who may not grasp their meaning and who will persist in seeing the justification of an action or object only in its obvious purpose. Have you ever read of, or even experienced, the deadly earnestness with which artist-vassals labor for art, their lord; of their sufferings on the score of language; or of what an overweening mistress form is? All this for something that has no aim or purpose! No, art does not bother about aims. Does anyone honestly believe that the artist would take upon himself or herself the thousand anxieties and feverish perplexities incident to creation if they intended to do nothing with their work but to teach the spectator a lesson, which they could just as well express in a couple of facile phrases, or one or two historical examples or a few well-taken photographs? The only answer to this can be an emphatic negative. Being an artist means wrestling with the expression of the hidden life of human beings in order that it may be given existence; nothing more. It is the image of the divine creation, of which it is said that it has made things *ut sint* [that they may be].

The liturgy does the same thing. It too, with endless care, with all the seriousness of the child and the strict consciousness of the great artist, has toiled to express in a thousand forms the sacred, God-given life of the soul to no other purpose than that the soul may therein have its existence and live its life. The liturgy has laid down the serious rules of the sacred game which the soul plays before God. If we are desirous of touching bottom in this mystery, it is the Spirit of fire and of holy discipline "who has knowledge of the world" (Responsory at Terce, Pentecost) — the Holy Ghost — who has ordained the game which the eternal Wisdom plays before the heavenly Father in the church, its kingdom on earth. And its delight is in this way "to be with the children of men."

Only those who are not scandalized by this understand what the liturgy means. From the very first every type of rationalism has turned against it. The practice of the liturgy means that by the help of grace, under the guidance of the church, we grow into living works of art before God, with no other aim or purpose than that of living and existing in his sight; it means fulfilling God's word and "becoming as little children"; it means foregoing maturity with all its purposefulness, and confining oneself to play, as David did when he danced before the Ark. It may, of course, happen that those extremely clever people, who merely by being grown up have lost all spiritual youth and spontaneity, will misunderstand this and gibe at it. David probably had to face the derision of Michal.

It is in this very aspect of the liturgy that its didactic aim is to be found — that of teaching the soul not to see purposes everywhere, not to be too conscious of the end it wishes to attain, not to be desirous of being over-clever and grown-up, but to understand simplicity in life. The soul must learn to abandon, at least in prayer, the restlessness of purposeful activity; it must learn to waste time for the sake of God, and to be prepared for the sacred game with sayings and thoughts and gestures, without always immediately asking "why?" and "wherefore?" It must learn not to be continually yearning to do something, to attack something, to accomplish something useful, but to play the divinely ordained game of the liturgy in liberty and beauty and holy joy before God.

In the end, eternal life will be its fulfillment. Will the people who do not understand the liturgy be pleased to find that the heavenly consummation is an eternal song of praise? Will they not rather associate themselves with those other industrious people who consider that such an eternity will be both boring and unprofitable?

The Spirit of the Liturgy, pages 176–184 (1918)

The Seriousness of the Liturgy

The church has not built up the *Opus Dei* for the pleasure of forming beautiful symbols, choice language and graceful, stately gestures; she has done it — in so far as it is not completely devoted to the worship of God — for the sake of our desperate spiritual need. It is to give expression to the events of the Christian's inner life: the assimilation, through the Holy Ghost, of the life of the creature unto the life of God in Christ; the actual and genuine rebirth of the creature into a new existence; the development and nourishment of this life, its stretching forth from God in the Blessed Sacrament and the means of grace, toward God in prayer and sacrifice. All this takes place in the continual mystical renewal of Christ's life in the course of the ecclesiastical year. The fulfillment of all these processes by the set forms of language, gesture and instruments, the revelation, teaching, accomplishment and acceptance by the faithful, together constitute the liturgy. We see, then, that it is primarily concerned with reality, with the approach of a real creature to a real God, and with the profoundly real and serious matter of redemption. There is here no question of creating beauty but of finding salvation for sin-stricken humanity. Here truth is at stake, and the fate of the soul, and real — yes, ultimately the only real — life. All this must be revealed, expressed, sought after, found and imparted by every possible means and method; when this is accomplished, lo! it is turned into beauty.

This is not a matter for amazement, since the principle at work here is the principle of truth and of mastery over form. The interior element has been expressed clearly and truthfully, the whole superabundance of life has found its utterance and the fathomless profundities have been plainly mapped out. It is only to be expected that a gleam of the utmost splendor should shine forth at such a manifestation of truth.

For us, however, the liturgy must chiefly be regarded from the standpoint of salvation. We should steadfastly endeavor to convince ourselves of its truth and its importance in our lives. When we recite the prayers and psalms of the liturgy, we are to praise God, nothing more. When we assist at Holy Mass, we must know that we are close to the fount of all grace. When we are present at an ordination, the significance of the proceedings must lie for us in the fact that the grace of God has taken possession of a fragment of human life. We are not concerned here with the question of powerfully symbolic gestures, as if we were in a spiritual theater, but we have to see that our real souls should approach a little nearer to the real God, for the sake of all our most personal, profoundly serious affairs.

For it is only thus that perception of liturgical beauty will be vouchsafed to us. It is only when we participate in liturgical action with the earnestness begotten of deep personal interest that we become aware why, and in what perfection, this vital essence is revealed.

The degree of perception varies according to our aesthetic sensitivity. Perhaps it will merely be a pleasant feeling of which we are not even particularly conscious, of the profound appropriateness of both language and actions for the expression of spiritual realities, a sensation of quiet spontaneity, a consciousness that everything is right and exactly as it should be. Then perhaps an offertory suddenly flashes in upon us, so that it gleams before us like a jewel; or bit by bit the whole sweep of the Mass is revealed, just as from out of the vanishing mist the peaks and summits and slopes of a mountain chain stand out in relief, shining and clear, so that we imagine we are looking at them for the first time. Or it may be that in the midst of prayer the soul will be pervaded by that gentle, blithe gladness which rises into sheer rapture. Perhaps the book will sink from our hands while, penetrated with awe, we taste the meaning of utter and blissful tranquility, conscious that the final and eternal verities which satisfy all longing have here found their perfect expression.

But these moments are fleeting, and we must be content to accept them as they come or are sent.

On the whole, however, and as far as everyday life is concerned, this precept holds good: "Seek first the kingdom of God and his justice, and all else shall be added to you" — all else, even the glorious experience of beauty.

The Spirit of the Liturgy, pages 196–198 (1918)

Chapter 9

Sacred Signs

The Symbolism of the Liturgy

A symbol may be said to originate when that which is interior and spiritual finds expression in that which is exterior and material. But it does not originate when (as in allegory) a spiritual element is by general consent coupled with a material substance as, for instance, the image of the scales with the idea of justice. Rather, the spiritual element must transpose itself into material terms because it is vital and essential that it do so. Thus the body is the natural emblem of the soul, and a spontaneous physical movement will typify a spiritual event. The symbol proper is circumscribed; it may be further distinguished by the total inability of the form selected as a medium of expression to represent anything else whatever. It must be expressed in clear and precise terms and therefore, when it has fulfilled the usual conditions, must be universally comprehensible. A genuine symbol is occasioned by the spontaneous expression of an actual and particular spiritual condition. At the same time, like a work of art, it must rise above the purely individual plane. It must not merely express isolated spiritual elements, but deal with life and the soul in the abstract.

Consequently when a symbol has been created, it often enjoys widespread currency and becomes universally comprehensible and significant. The auspicious collaboration of both types of temperament [i.e., the disposition which sees the physical and the spiritual spheres as separate, and that which sees them as united] is essential to the creation of a symbol, in which the spiritual and the physical elements must be united in perfect harmony. At the same time it is the task of the spiritual element to watch over and determine every stroke of the modeling, to sort and sift with a sure hand, to measure off and weigh together delicately and discreetly, in order that the given matter may be given its corresponding and appropriate form. The more clearly and completely the spiritual content is cast in its material mold, the more valuable is the symbol thus produced, and the more worthy it is of its name, because it then loses its connection with the solitary incident which occasioned it and becomes a universal possession. The greater the depth of life from which it has sprung, and the greater the degree of clarity and of conviction which has contributed to its formation, the more true this is in proportion.

    The power of symbol-building was at work when the fundamental rules governing social intercourse were laid down. From it are derived those forms by which one person signifies to another interest or reverence, in which are externally expressed the inward happenings of civil and political life and the like. Further — and in this connection it is specially significant — it is the origin of those gestures which convey a spiritual meaning; the man or woman who is moved by emotion will kneel, bow, clasp hands or impose them, stretch forth their arms, strike their breast, make an offering of something and so on. These elementary gestures are capable of richer development and expansion, or else of amalgamation. They are the source of the manifold ritual actions such as the kiss of peace or the blessing. Or it may be that certain ideas are expressed in corresponding movements; thus belief in the mystery of absolution is shown by the sign of the cross. Finally, a whole series of such movements may be coordinated. This gives rise to religious action by which a richly developed spiritual element — e.g., a sacrifice — succeeds in attaining external and symbolic expression. It is when that form of self-experience which has been described above is extended to objects which lie outside the personal province that the material concrete factor enters into the symbol. Material objects are used to reinforce the expressiveness of the body and its movements and at the same time form an extension of the permanent bodily powers. For instance, in a sacrifice the victim is offered not only by the hands, but in a vessel or dish. The smooth surface of the dish emphasizes the expressive motion of the hand; it forms a wide and open plane, displayed before the Godhead, throwing into powerful relief the upward straining line of the arm. Or again, as it rises, the smoke of the incense enhances the aspiration expressed by the upturned hands and gaze of those who are at prayer. The candle, with its slender, soaring, tapering column tipped with flame, consuming itself as it burns, typifies the idea of sacrifice which is voluntarily offered in lofty spiritual serenity.

Both the aforementioned types of temperament cooperate in the creation of symbol. The one, with its apprehension of the affinity between the spiritual and the physical, provides the material for the primary hypothesis essential to the creation of the symbol. The other, by its power of distinction and its objectiveness, brings to the symbol lucidity and form. They both, however, find in the liturgy the problems peculiar to their temperament. Because they have shared together in the creation of the liturgical symbol, both are capable of overcoming these difficulties — as soon, that is, as they are in some way convinced of the binding value of the liturgy.

The former type, then, must abandon their exaggerated spirituality, admit the existence of the relationship between the spiritual and the physical, and freely avail themselves of the wealth of liturgical symbolism. They must give up their reserve and the Puritanism which prompts them to oppose the expression of the spiritual in material terms, and must instead take the material as a medium of lively expression. This will add a new warmth and depth to the emotional and spiritual experience.

The latter type must endeavor to stem the extravagance of sensation and to bind the vague and ephemeral elements into clear-cut forms. It is of the highest importance that they should realize that the liturgy is entirely free from any subjection to matter, and that all the natural elements in the liturgy are entirely re-cast as ritual forms. For people of this type the symbolizing power of the liturgy becomes a school of measure and of spiritual restraint.

People who really live by the liturgy will come to learn that the bodily movements, the actions and the material objects which it employs are all of the highest significance. It offers great opportunities of expression, of knowledge and of spiritual experience; it is emancipating in its action, and capable of presenting a truth far more strongly and convincingly than can the mere word of mouth.

The Spirit of the Liturgy, pages 167–170 (1918)

The Altar as Table

The altar is the threshold to God's immanence. Through Christ, God ceased to be the Unknown, the Inaccessible One; he turned to us, came to us and became one of us in order that we might go to him and become one with him. The altar is the frontier, the border where God comes to us and we go to him in a most special way.

At this point a few remarks are in order about the images used to express sacred mysteries. The images unlock the storehouse of God's riches and they help us to concentrate on particular aspects of divine reality with all our power. When we consider the altar as a threshold, we see one particular trait, leaving out of consideration any other, such as that expressed by the concept *table*. The images used are necessarily taken from objects of our own experience. But, since we are not cut off from God and his life as is one room in a house from another, we must not put too much emphasis on the inability of images adequately to express divine realities. If we do, we lose something precious, something essential. Images are not makeshifts, handy for children and for the vulgar crowd, which the cultured elite, wrestling with pure concepts, should despise. When Jacob, Abraham's grandson, woke from his great dream, he cried: "How terrible is this place! This is no other than the house of God, and the gate of heaven" (Genesis 28:17). And Saint John writes: ". . . and behold, a door standing open in heaven, and the former voice, which I had heard as of a trumpet speaking with me, said, 'Come up hither, and I will show thee the things that must come to pass hereafter'" (Revelation 4:1).

Now if we are to say that *door* is here only a figure of speech suggesting that God is invisible yet near, that no one can reach him but he can draw us to himself, we would be correct, but we would fail to grasp the basic meaning of John's words. Saint John wrote *door* because he meant *door* — and not only poetically. The intellect may attempt to express in concepts and sentences all that the image *door* implies, but such concepts are mere props to the essential. The truth is the other way around: it is the image that is the reality; the mind can only attempt to plumb it. The image is richer than the thought; hence, the act by which we comprehend an image — gazing — is richer, more profound, more vital and storied than the thought. People today are, if the word may be permitted, over-conceptualistic. We have lost the art of reading images and parables, of enacting symbols. We could relearn some of this by encouraging and practicing the power of vision, a power which has been neglected for too long.

To return to our subject: the mystery of the altar is only partially suggested by the image of the threshold; altar is also table.

The presentiment of a sacred table at which not only humanity but also divinity takes its place is to be found in the religions of all peoples. Everywhere the pious believer places gifts upon an altar so that the godhead may accept them. The idea that these gifts belong to the godhead and no longer to humanity is conveyed by their destruction or withdrawal from human use. The body of the sacrificial animal is burned, the drink poured out upon the ground. The immolation symbolizes what is contained in the process of death: the passing over to the other side, to the realm of the divine.

A second process is often related to the first. Not everything is given over; part is retained — or rather returned (for what was destroyed represented the whole) — now to be enjoyed by the offerers. Thus godhead and believers are nourished by the same sacred food. Behind this concept lies one still more profound: one's offering stands for oneself, is really oneself; the true offering is human sacrifice. Again, the offering stands for the godhead itself; true nourishment is divine life.

From a certain standpoint these conceptions are very profound, although closer examination reveals that they have sunk into gloom, worldliness and animalism. The godhead lives from the life of human beings — of a tribe, a people; on the other hand, the believer sees in his godhead the spiritual mainspring of his own life and that of his clan, tribe, people. Divinity has need of humanity and humanity of divinity, for in the final analysis they are the same; sacrifice is the constantly renewed process of this union.

Such conceptions are totally absent from the Old Testament. The God to whose altar offerings are brought is neither the vital principle of a people nor the secret of the world's vitality, but Creator and Lord of all that is. The offering is an acknowledgment of his lordship; it in no way affects his potency, but is simply a recognition that all things are his, and that people may dispose of them only with God's permission. Strictly speaking, the animal from the flock should be slaughtered only before the altar — not because God has any need of its blood, but because all life is his property; the harvest should be consumed only before the altar, since everything that bears its seed within itself belongs to God. The idea is expressed in the sacrifice of livestock and in the offering of the field's first fruits. Only then does humanity receive herd and harvest back from the altar for its own use.

The altar is the table to which the heavenly Father invites us. Through salvation we have become sons and daughters of God, and his house is ours. At the altar we enjoy the intimate community of his sacred table. From his hands we receive the "bread of heaven," the word of truth, and — far excelling all imaginable gifts — his own incarnate Son, the living Christ (see John 6). What is given us, then, is at once corporal reality and sentient truth, Life and Person, in short — Gift.

If we ask whether at the sacred table God too receives something, whether the age-old presentiment of a real community of table between God and humanity is not also fulfilled in the clean air of Christian faith, the answer is not easy. Fear of being irreverent makes us cautious. However, we can point to a mystery that fills the letters of Saint Paul and appears also in the farewell speeches of the Gospel of Saint John. The fruit of the divine sojourn on earth is salvation. This means not only our forgiveness and justification but also that the world is *brought home* to the Father. It means not only that we return to God in love and obedience but that we are received into divine life — and through us, the world in all its reality. God desires this. When we are told that he loves us, this does not mean that he is merely benevolent toward us; the word is meant in all its abundance.

God longs for us. He wants to have his creatures close to him. When Christ cried from the cross, "I thirst," a dying man's bodily torment was indeed expressed, but much more besides (John 19:28). Similarly at Jacob's well, when the disciples encouraged Jesus to eat the food they had brought, he replied: "My food is to do the will of him who sent me, to accomplish his work" (John 4:34). Mysterious hungering and thirsting, this — the hunger and thirst of God! Saint Augustine writes that receiving the eucharist does not so much mean that we partake of the divine life offered us, as that the divine life draws us into itself. These thoughts should not be pressed too far, for they are holy. It is important, however, to know that a mystery of divine-human love and communion does exist and that it is realized at the altar.

Meditations Before Mass, pages 53–57 (1939)

The Sign of the Cross

When we cross ourselves, let it be with a real sign of the cross. Instead of a small cramped gesture that gives no notion of its meaning, let us make a large unhurried sign from forehead to breast, from shoulder to shoulder, consciously feeling how it includes the whole of us — our thoughts, our attitudes, our body and soul, every part of us at once — how it consecrates and sanctifies us.

It does so because it is the sign of the universe and the sign of our redemption. On the cross Christ redeemed humankind. By the cross he sanctifies us to the last shred and fiber of our being. We make the sign of the cross before we pray to collect and compose ourselves and to fix our minds and hearts and wills upon God. We make it when we finish praying in order that we may hold fast the gift we have received from God. In temptations we sign ourselves to be strengthened; in dangers, to be protected. The cross is signed upon us in blessings in order that the fullness of God's life may flow into the soul and fructify and sanctify us wholly.

Think of these things when you make the sign of the cross. It is the holiest of all signs. Make a large cross, taking time, thinking about what you do. Let it take in your whole being — body, soul, mind, will, thoughts, feelings, your doing and not-doing — and by signing it with the cross strengthen and consecrate the whole in the strength of Christ, in the name of the triune God.

Sacred Signs, pages 13–14 (1929)

The Hands

Every part of the body is an expressive instrument of the soul. The soul does not inhabit the body as a person inhabits a house. It lives and works in each member, each fiber, and reveals itself in the body's every line, contour and movement. But the soul's chief instruments and clearest mirrors are the face and the hands.

Of the face that is obviously true. But if you will watch other people (or yourself), you will notice how instantly every slightest feeling — pleasure, surprise, suspense — shows in the hand. A quick lifting of the hand or a flicker of the fingers says far more than words. By comparison with a language so natural and expressive the spoken word is clumsy. Next to the face, the part of the body fullest of mind is the hand. It is a hard, strong tool for work, a ready weapon of attack and defense; but also, with its delicate structure and network of innumerable nerves, it is adaptable, flexible and highly sensitive. It is a skillful workmanlike contrivance for the soul by which to make itself known. It is also an organ of receptivity for matter from outside ourselves. For when we clasp the extended hand of a stranger are we not receiving from a foreign source the confidence, pleasure, sympathy or sorrow that it conveys?

So it could not but be that in prayer, where the soul has so much to say, so much to learn from God, where it gives itself to him and receives him to itself, that the hand takes on expressive forms.

When we enter into ourselves and the soul is alone with God our hands closely interlock, finger clasped in finger, in a gesture of compression and control. It is as if we would prevent the inner current from escaping by conducting it from hand to hand and so back again to God who is within us, holding it there. It is as if we were collecting all our forces to keep guard over the hidden God, so that he who is mine and I who am his should be left alone together. Our hands take the same position when some dire need or pain weighs heavily on us and threatens to break out. Hand then locks in hand and the soul struggles with itself until it gets control and grows quiet again.

But when we stand in God's presence in heartfelt reverence and humility the open hands are laid together palm against palm in a sign of steadfast subjection and obedient homage, as if to say that the words we speak are in good order, and that we are ready and attentive to hear the words of God. Or it may be a sign of inner surrender. These hands, our weapons of defense, are laid, as it were, tied and bound together between the hands of God.

In moments of jubilant thanksgiving when the soul is entirely open to God with every reserve done away with and every passage of its instrument unstopped, and it flows at the full outward and upward, the hands are uplifted and spread apart with the palms up to let the river of the spirit stream out unhindered and to receive in turn the water for which it thirsts. So too when we long for God and cry out to him.

Finally, when sacrifice is called for and we gather together all we are and all we have and offer ourselves to God with full consent, then we lay our arms over our [heart] and make with them the sign of the cross.

There is greatness and beauty in this language of the hands. The church tells us that God has given us our hands in order that we may carry our souls in them. The church is fully in earnest in the use it makes of the language of gesture. It speaks through this language its inmost mind, and God gives ear to this mode of speaking.

Our hands may also indicate the goods we lack — our unchecked impulses, our distractions and other faults. Let us hold them as the church directs and see to it that there is a real correspondence between the interior and exterior attitude.

In matters such as this we are on delicate ground. We would prefer not to talk about things of this order. Something within us objects. Let us then avoid all empty and unreal talk and concentrate more carefully on the actual doing. That is a form of speech by which the plain realities of the body say to God what its soul means and intends.

Sacred Signs, pages 15–18 (1929)

Standing

The respect we owe to the infinite God requires of us a bearing suited to such presence. The sense that we have of the greatness of his being and, in his eyes, of the slightness of our own, is shown outwardly by our kneeling down to make ourselves small. But reverence has another way of expressing itself. When you are sitting down to rest or chat and someone to whom you owe respect comes in and turns to speak to you, at once you stand up and remain standing as long as that person is speaking and you are answering him or her. Why do we do this?

In the first place, to stand up means that we are in possession of ourselves. Instead of sitting relaxed and at ease we take hold of ourselves, we stand, as it were, at attention, geared and ready for action. People on their feet can come or go at once. They can take an order in an instant, or carry out an assignment the moment they are shown what is wanted.

Standing is the other side of reverence toward God. Kneeling is the side of worship in rest and quietness; standing is the side of vigilance and action. It is the respect of the servant in attendance, of the soldier on duty.

When the good news of the gospel is proclaimed, we stand up. Godparents stand when in the child's place they make the solemn profession of faith; children stand when they renew these promises at their first communion. Bridegroom and bride stand when they bind themselves at the altar to be faithful to their marriage vow. On these and like occasions we stand up.

Even when we are praying alone, to pray standing may more forcibly express our inward state. The early Christians stood by preference. The *Orante,* in the familiar catacomb representation, stands in her long flowing robes of a woman of rank and prays with outstretched hands, in perfect freedom and perfect obedience, quietly attending to the word and in readiness to perform it with joy.

We may feel at times a sort of constraint in kneeling. One feels freer standing up, and in that case standing is the right position. But stand up straight, not leaning, both feet on the ground, knees firm, not slackly bent, upright, in control. Prayer made thus is both free and obedient, both reverent and serviceable.

Meditations Before Mass, pages 21–23 (1939)

Doors

Every time we enter a church, if we but notice it, a question is put to us. Why does a church have doors? It seems a foolish question. Naturally, to go in by. Yes, but doors are not necessary — only a doorway. An opening with a board partition to close it off would be a cheap and practical convenience for letting people out and in. But the door serves more than a practical use; it is a reminder.

When you step through the doorway of a church you are leaving the outer world behind and entering an inner world. The outside world is a fair place abounding in life and activity, but also a place with a mingling of the base and ugly. It is a sort of marketplace, crossed and recrossed by all and sundry. Perhaps "unholy" is not quite the word for it, yet there is something profane about the world. Behind the church door is an inner place, separated from the market place, a silent, consecrated and holy spot. It is very certain that the whole world is the work of God and his gift to us, that we may meet him anywhere, that everything we receive is from God's hands and, when received religiously, is holy. Nevertheless, people have always felt that certain precincts were in a special manner set apart and dedicated to God.

Between the outer and inner world are the doors. They are the barriers between the marketplace and the sanctuary, between what belongs to the world at large and what has become consecrated to God. And the door warns the men and women who open it to go inside that they must now leave behind the thoughts, wishes and cares which here are out of place: their curiosity, their vanity, their worldly interests, their secular self. "Make yourself clean. The ground you tread is holy ground."

Do not rush through the doors. Let us take time to open our hearts to their meaning and pause a moment beforehand to make our entering-in a fully intended and recollected act.

The doors have something else to say. Notice how as you cross the threshold you unconsciously lift your head and your eyes, and how as you survey the great interior space of the church there also takes place in you an inward expansion and enlargement. Its great width and height have an analogy to infinity and eternity. A church is a similitude of the heavenly dwelling place of God. Mountains are higher and the wide blue sky outside stretches immeasurably farther, but whereas outside space is unconfined and formless, the portion of space set aside for the church has been formed, fashioned and designed at every point with God in view. The long pillared aisles, the width and solidity of the walls, the high arched and vaulted roof bring home to us that this is God's house and the seat of his hidden presence.

It is the doors that admit us to this mysterious place. Lay aside, they say, all that cramps and narrows, all that sinks the mind. Open your heart, lift up your eyes. Let your soul be free, for this is God's temple.

It is likewise the representation of you, yourself. For you, your soul and your body, are the living temple of God. Open up that temple, make it spacious, give it height.

Lift up your heads, O ye gates,
and be ye lifted up, ye everlasting doors,
and the King of Glory shall come in.

Heed the cry of the doors. Of small use to you is a house of wood and stone unless you yourself are God's living dwelling. The high arched gates may be lifted up and the portals parted wide, but unless the doors of your heart are open, how can the King of Glory enter in?

Sacred Signs, pages 37–40 (1929)

Candles

We stand in a double and contrary relationship to objects outside ourselves. We stand to the world and all its contents as when God brought the animals to the first man for him to name. Among them all Adam could find no companion. Between men and women and the rest of creation there is a barrier of difference which neither scientific knowledge nor moral depravity can remove or efface. They are of another make from every other creature. To other creatures they are foreign. Their kinship is with God.

On the other hand we are related to everything that exists in the world. Everywhere we feel somehow at home. The shapes, attitudes, movements of objects all speak to us; all are a means of communication. It is the incessant occupation of the human soul to express through them its own interior life, and to make them serve as its signs and symbols. Every notable form we come across strikes us as expressing something in our own nature, and reminds us of ourselves.

This feeling of our connection with things is the source of metaphor and simile. We are profoundly estranged from, yet mysteriously connected to, outside objects. They are not us, yet all that is or happens is an image of ourselves.

One of these image-objects strikes me, and I think most people, as having more than ordinary force and beauty. It is that of a lighted candle. There it rises, firmly fixed in the metal cup on the broad-based, long-shafted candlestick; spare and white, yet not wan; distinct against whatever background; consuming in the little flame that flickers above it the pure substance of the wax in softly shining light. It seems a symbol of selfless generosity. It stands unwavering in its place, so erect, so clear and disinterested, in perfect readiness to be of service. It stands, where it is well to stand, before God; it stands in an appointed place, self-consumed in light and warmth.

Yes, of course the candle is unconscious of what it does. It has no soul. But we can, however, give it a soul by making it an expression of our own attitude.

Stir up in yourself the same generous readiness to be used. "Lord, here I am." Let the clean, spare, serviceable candle bespeak your own attitude. Let your readiness grow into steadfast loyalty. Even as this candle, O Lord, would I stand in your presence.

Do not weaken in or try to evade your vocation. Persevere. Do not keep asking why and to what purpose. To be consumed in truth and love, in light and warmth, for God, is the profoundest purpose of human life.

Sacred Signs, pages 41–43 (1929)

Holy Water

Water is a mysterious thing. It is so clear and frictionless, so "modest," as Saint Francis calls it. It hardly pretends to any character of its own. It seems to have no other end or object than to be of service, to cleanse what is soiled and to refresh what is dry.

But at some time you must have gazed down into the still depth of a great body of water, and felt it tugging to draw you in, and had a glimpse of the strange and secret thing water is, and of the marvels, terrors and enticements that lurk in its depth. Or, at another time when it was whipped to a boiling torrent by a storm, you have heard it rushing and roaring, rushing and roaring, and watched the sucking vortex of a whirlpool and felt a force so grim and [dreadful] that you had to tear your thoughts away.

Water is indeed a strange element. On the one hand smooth and transparent, as if it hardly existed in its own right, ready at hand to wash away dirt and satisfy thirst; and on the other a restless, foundationless, enigmatic force that entices us in to destruction. It is a proper image for the secret ground-force from which life issues and back into which death recalls it. It is an apt image for this life of ours that looks so clear and is so inexplicable.

It is plain why the church uses water as the sign and the bearer of the divine life of grace. We emerge from the waters of baptism into a new life, born again of water and the Holy Spirit. In those same waters the old individual was destroyed and put to death.

With this element that yields no answer to our questioning — with this transparent, frictionless, fecund fluid, this symbol and means of the supernatural life of grace — we make on ourselves, from shoulder to shoulder, the sign of the cross.

By her consecration of it, the church has freed water from the dark powers that sleep in it. This is not a form of language. Anyone whose perceptions have not been blunted must be aware of the powers of natural magic inherent in water. Are they only natural powers? Is there not present also a dark and preternatural power? In nature, for all her richness and beauty, there is something demonic. City life has so deadened our senses that we have lost our perception of it. But the church knows it is there. She exorcises out of water those spirits that are at enmity with God. She blesses it and asks God to make of it a vehicle of his grace. Therefore the Christians when they enter the church moisten forehead, breast and shoulders, all their person, with the clean and cleansing water in order to make clean their soul. It is a pleasing custom that brings grace and nature freed from sin, and human beings, who so long for cleanness, into the unity of the sign of the cross.

At evening also we sign ourselves in holy water. Night, as the proverb says, is no friend to humans. Our human nature is formed and fashioned for light. Just before we give ourselves over into the power of sleep and darkness and the light of day and consciousness is extinguished, there is the satisfaction of making the sign of the cross on ourselves with holy water. Holy water is the symbol of nature set free from sin. May God protect us from every darkness! At morning when we emerge again out of sleep, darkness and unconsciousness, and life begins afresh, we do the same thing. But in the morning it is to remind ourselves of that holy water from which we have issued into the light of Christ. The soul redeemed and nature redeemed encounter one another in the sign of the cross.

Sacred Signs, pages 45–48 (1929)

Bread and Wine

Seeing God, loving God, by consciously turning toward him with our minds and wills, though a real union, is yet not a union of being with him. It is not only our minds and our wills that strive to possess God. As the psalm says, "My heart and my flesh are athirst for the living God." Only then shall we be at rest when our whole being is joined to his, not by any mingling or confusion of natures, for creature and creator are forever distinct; to suppose otherwise would be as nonsensical as it is presumptuous. Nevertheless, besides the union of simple love and knowledge, there is another union — that of life and being.

We desire, are compelled to desire, this union, and scripture and liturgy place upon our lips words that give profound expression to our longing. As the body desires food and drink, just so closely does our individual life desire to be united with God. We hunger and thirst after God. It is not enough for us to know him and to love him. We would clasp him, draw him to ourselves, hold him fast and, bold as it sounds, we would take him into ourselves as we do our necessary food and drink, and thereby still and satisfy our hunger to the full.

The liturgy of Corpus Christi repeats to us these words of Christ: "As the living Father hath sent me, and I live by the Father, the same shall also live by me." Those are the words. For us to offer such a claim as a thing due to us of right would border on blasphemy. But since it is God that speaks, we inwardly assent and believe.

Let us not presume that the bread and wine in any way efface the boundary between creature and Creator. In deepest reverence, and yet without fear, let us acknowledge the longing which God himself has planted in us and rejoice in this gift of his exceeding goodness. "My flesh," Christ says to us, "is food indeed, and my blood is drink indeed. . . . He that eats my flesh and drinks my blood abides in me and I in him. . . . As the Father hath given me to have life in myself, so he that eats me, the same also shall live by me." To eat his flesh, to drink his blood, to eat him, to absorb into ourselves the living God — it is beyond any wish we might be capable of forming for ourselves, yet it satisfies to the full what we long for — of necessity long for — from the bottom of our souls.

Bread is food. It is wholesome, nourishing food for which we never lose our appetite. Under the form of bread God becomes for us the food of life. "We break a bread," writes Saint Ignatius of Antioch to the faithful at Ephesus, "we break a bread that is the food of immortality." By this food our being is so nourished with God himself that we exist in him and he in us.

Wine is drink. To be exact, it is more than drink, more than a liquid like water that merely quenches thirst. "Wine that makes glad the heart" is the biblical expression. The purpose of wine is not only to quench thirst, but also to give pleasure and satisfaction and exhilaration. "My cup, how goodly it is, how plenteous!" Literally, how intoxicating, though not in the sense of drinking to excess. Wine possesses a sparkle, a perfume, a vigor, that expands and clears the imagination. Under the form of wine Christ gives us his divine blood. It is no plain and sober draught. It was bought at a great price, at a divinely excessive price. *Sanguis Christi, inebria me,* prays Saint Ignatius, that knight of the burning heart. In one of the antiphons for the feast of Saint Agnes, the blood of Christ is called a mystery of ineffable beauty. "I have drawn milk and honey from his lips and his blood hath given fair color to my cheeks."

For our sake Christ became bread and wine, food and drink. We make bold to eat him and to drink him. This bread gives us solid and substantial strength. This wine bestows courage, joy out of all earthly measure, sweetness, beauty, limitless enlargement and perception. It brings life in intoxicating excess, both to possess and to impart.

Sacred Signs, pages 65–68 (1929)

Blessing

He alone can bless that has the power. He alone is able to bless who is able to create. God alone can bless.

God, when he blesses his creatures, looks upon them and calls them by their name; he brings all his powerful love to bear upon the pith and center of their being and pours out from his hand the power of fruitfulness, the power of growth and the increase of health and goodness. "I will keep my eyes upon you and make you to increase."

Only God can bless. Blessing is the disposition to be made of what a thing is or effects. It is the word of power of the Master of Creation. It is the promise and assurance of the Lord of Providence. Blessing bestows a happy destiny.

Nietzsche's remark, that instead of favors we should confer blessings, is the saying of a rebel. He well understood his own meaning. God only can bless since God only is the master of life. By our nature we are petitioners. The contrary of blessing is cursing. A curse is a sentence and a seal of mischief. It is, like blessing, a judgment imprinted upon the forehead and the heart. It shuts off the sources of life.

God has imparted a portion of his power to bless and to curse to those whose vocation it is to create life. Parents possess this power. "The blessing of the father establishes the houses of the children." Priests possess it. As parents engender natural life, so the priest begets the supernatural life of grace. To give life is the nature and office of both.

Those also may attain to the power of blessing who no longer seek themselves but in perfect simplicity of heart will to be the servant of the one who has life in himself.

But the power to bless is always and only from God. It fails wholly if we assume it of ourselves. By nature we are petitioners; we are blessers only by God's grace — just as we have the virtue of authority, of effectual command, only by God's grace.

What applies to blessing also applies to cursing: "The mother's curse roots up the foundations of the children's houses," that is to say, of their life and their well-being.

All the forms of nature are prefigurations of grace. The power of effectual blessing, the power which the blessing actually conveys — the real, essential power, of which our natural life is but a figure — is God's own life. It is with himself that God blesses. The divine life is begotten by God's blessing. By it we are made sharers in the divine nature by a pure gift, a grace, bestowed on us by Christ. So also the sign of the cross is a blessing in which God bestows himself upon us.

The power of divine blessings is merely lent to those who stand in God's stead. Fathers and mothers have it by the sacrament of Christian marriage. The priest has it by the sacrament of ordination. By virtue of the sacrament of baptism and the sacrament of confirmation — which makes us kings and priests to God — there is given to those "who love God with all their heart and all their mind and all their strength and their neighbors as themselves" the power to bless with God's own life. To each of these the power of blessing is given with such difference as the nature of their apostleship determines.

The visible representation of blessing is the hand. By its position and action it indicates the purpose of the blessing. In confirmation it is laid on the head so that the Spirit which has its source in God may flow through it. When the hand signs the cross on the forehead or breast it is in order that the divine plenitude may be poured out unstintingly. The hand, as it is the instrument of making and shaping, is also the instrument of spending and giving.

Finally, there is the blessing given not by the hand but by the All-Holy himself with the sacramental body of Christ. Let it be bestowed in profound reverence and subjection to the mystery.

Sacred Signs, pages 81–84 (1929)

Time Sanctified

Though each hour of the day has its own character, three hours stand out from the rest — morning, evening and, halfway between them, noonday — and have an aspect distinctly their own. These three hours the church has consecrated.

Morning.

Of them all the morning hour wears the most shining face. It possesses the energy and brightness of a beginning. Mysteriously, each morning we are born again. We emerge out of sleep refreshed, renewed, with an invigorating sense of being alive. This newly infused feeling of our existence turns to a prayer of thanksgiving for life to him who gave it. With an impulse to action born of fresh energy we think of the day ahead and of the work to be done in it, and this impulse also becomes a prayer. We begin the day in God's name and strength and ask him to make our work a work for him.

This morning hour, when life reawakens and we are more keenly aware of our existence, when we begin the day with gratitude for our creation and turn to our work with fresh creative power, is a holy hour.

It is plain how much depends on this first hour. It is the day's beginning. The day may be started without a beginning. The day may be slipped into without thought or intention, but such a day, without purpose or character, hardly deserves the name. It is no more than a torn-off scrap of time. A day is a journey. One must decide which way one is going. It is also a work, and as such requires to be willed. A single day is the whole of life. The whole of life is like a day. Each day should have its own distinct character.

The morning hour exercises the will, directs the intention and sets our gaze wholly upon God.

Evening.

Evening also has its mystery. The mystery of evening is death. The day draws to a close and we make ready to enter the silence of sleep. The vigor which came with the morning has by evening run down, and what we seek then is rest. The secret note of death is sounded; and though our imaginations may be too crowded with the day's doings or too intent on tomorrow's plans for us to hear it distinctly, some perception of it, however remote, does reach us. There are evenings when we have very much the feeling that life is drawing on to the long night "wherein no one can work."

What matters is to have a right understanding of what death means. Dying is more than the end of life. Death is the last summons that life serves on us. Dying is the final, the all-decisive act. With individuals, as with nations, the events that precede extinction in themselves conclude and settle nothing. After the thing has happened it remains to be determined, by nations as by individuals, what is to be made of it, how it is to be regarded. The past event is neither good nor evil; in itself it is nothing. It is the face we put upon it, our way of viewing it, that makes it what it is. A great calamity, let us say, has overtaken a nation. The event has happened, but it is not over with. The nation may give way to despair. It may also think the matter through again, rejudge it and make a fresh start. Not until we have decided how to take it is the event, long past though it may be, completed. The deep significance of death is that it is the final sentence a person passes on his or her life. It has the definite character that person stamps upon it. When we come to die we must decide whether we will or will not once more take our whole life in hand, be sorry for all we have done amiss and plunge and recast it in the burning heat of repentance. We must decide whether we will or will not give God humble thanks for what was well done (to him be the honor!) and cast the whole upon God in entire abandonment. Or we may give way to despondency, and weakly and ignobly let life slip from us. In this case life comes to no conclusion; it merely, without shape or character, ceases to be.

The high art of dying is to accept the life that is leaving us, and by a single act of affirmation put it into God's hands.

Each evening we should practice the high art of giving life an effectual conclusion by reshaping the past and impressing it with a final validity and an eternal character. The evening hour is the hour of completion. We stand before God with the premonition of the day on which we shall stand before him face to face and give our final reckoning. We have a sense of the past being past, with its good and evil, its losses and waste. We place ourselves before God to whom all time, past or future, is the living present; before God who is able to restore to the penitent even what is lost. We think back over the day gone by. What was not well done contrition seizes upon and thinks anew. For what was well done we give God humble thanks, sincerely taking no credit for ourselves. What we are uncertain about, or failed to accomplish, the whole sorry remnant, we sink in entire abandonment into God's all-powerful love.

Midday.

In the morning we have a lively and agreeable sense that life is starting and is on the increase; then obstacles arise and we are slowed. By noon for a short while we seem to stand quite still. A little later our sense of life declines; we grow weary, recover a little, and then subside into the quiescence of night.

Halfway between the rising and setting sun, when the day is at its height, comes a breathing space, a brief and wonderful moment. The future is not pressing and we do not look ahead; the day is not yet declining and we do not look back. It is a pause, but not of weariness; our strength and energy are still at the full. Noonday is the pure present. It looks beyond itself, but not into space or time. It looks upon eternity.

Noon is a profound moment. In the stir and extroversion of a city it passes unperceived. But in the country, among cornfields and quiet pastures, when the horizon is glowing with heat, we perceive what a deep moment it is. We stand still and time falls away. Eternity confronts us. Every hour reminds us of eternity; but noon is its close neighbor. Time waits and holds its peace. The day is at the full and time is the pure present.

The day being at its height and eternity close by, let us attend to it and give it entrance. In the distance the Angelus, breaking the noontide silence, reminds us of our redemption. "In the beginning was the Word and the Word was with God. . . . The angel of the Lord brought the message to Mary, and she conceived of the Holy Ghost. Behold the handmaid of the Lord, be it done unto me according to thy will. . . . And the Word became flesh and dwelt among us."

At the noon hour, in the fullness of time, a member of the human race on whom the fullness had come, stood and waited. Mary did not hurry to meet it. She looked neither before nor after. The fullness of time, the simple present, the moment that gives entrance to eternity, was upon her. She waited. Eternity leaned over; the angel spoke, and the eternal Word took flesh in her pure [heart].

Now in our day the Angelus proclaims the mystery. Each noonday, for each Christian soul, the noonday of humanity is again present. At every moment of time the fullness of time is audible. At all times our life is close neighbor to eternity. We should always hold ourselves in that quietude that attends upon and is open to eternity. But since the noise of living is so loud, let us pause at least at noon, at the hour the church has sanctified, and set aside the business we are engaged in. Let us stand in silence and listen to the angel of the Lord proclaiming that "while the earth lay in deepest silence the eternal Lord leapt down from his royal throne" — into the course of history once only, but since then at every moment into the human soul.

Sacred Signs, pages 93–99 (1929)

The Name of God

Human perception has been dulled. We have lost our awareness of some deep and subtle things, among them the zest for words. Words have for us now only a surface existence. They have lost their power to shock and startle. They have been reduced to a fleeting image, to a thin tinkle of sound.

Actually, a word is the subtle body of a spirit. Two things meet and find expression in a word: the substance of the object that makes the impact and that portion of our spirit that responds to that particular object. At least these two ought to go into the making of words, and did when the first human being made them.

In one of the early chapters of the first book of the Bible we are told that "God brought the animals to Adam to see what he would call them." A human being who had the ability to see and a mind open to impressions looked through the outward form into the inner essence and spoke the name. The name was the response made by the human soul to the soul of the creature. Something in the human being, that particular part of itself that corresponded to the nature of that particular creature, stirred in answer, since humans are the epitome and point of union of creation. These two things, or rather the double thing — the nature of things outside and a person's interior correspondence with them — being brought into lively contact found utterance in the name.

In a name a particle of the universe is locked with a particle of human consciousness, so when Adam spoke the name, the image of the actual object appeared in his mind together with the sound he had made in response to it. The name was the secret sign which opened to him the world without and the world within himself.

Words are names. Speech is the noble act of giving things the names that fit them. The thing as it is in its nature and the soul as it is in its nature were divinely intended to sound in union.

But the inward connection between human beings and the rest of creation was interrupted. Humans sinned, and the bond was torn apart. Things became alien, even hostile, to them. Their eyes lost the clearness of their vision. They looked at nature with greed, with the desire to master it and with the shifty glance of the guilty. Things shut their real nature from them. They asserted themselves so successfully that their own nature eluded them. When they lost their childlike vision, their soul fell away from them, and with it their wisdom and their strength.

With the loss of the true name was broken that vital union between the two parts of creation, the human and the non-human, which in God's intention were to be indissolubly joined in the bonds of peace. Only some fragmentary image, some obscure, confused echo, still reaches us; if on occasion we do hear a word that is really a name, we stop short and try but cannot quite catch its import, and we are left puzzled and troubled with the painful sensation that paradise is lost.

But in our day even the sense that paradise is lost is lost. We are too superficial to be distressed by the loss of meaning, though we are more and more glib about the surface sense. We pass words from mouth to mouth as we do money from hand to hand, with no more attention to what they were meant to convey than to the inscription on the coins. The value-mark is all we notice. Words signify something, but reveal nothing. Far from promoting the intercourse between people and nature, they clatter out of us like coins from a cash register and with much the same consciousness of their value as the machine has.

Once in a while we are shocked into attention. A word, perhaps in a book, may strike us with all its original force. The black and white signs grow luminous. We hear the voice of the thing named. There is the same astonished impact, the same intellectual insight, as in the primitive encounter. We are carried out of ourselves into the far depth of time when God summoned the man to his first work of word-making. But too soon we are back where we were and the cash register goes clicking on.

It may have been the name of God that we thus met face to face. Remembering how words came to be, it is plain enough to us why the faithful under the Old Law never uttered the word, and substituted for it the word Lord. What made the Jews the peculiar and elect nation is that they, with more immediacy than any other people, perceived the reality and nearness of God, and had a stronger sense of his greatness, his transcendence and his fecundity. His name had been revealed to them by Moses. *The one who is,* that is his name. The one who is being in itself, needing nothing, self-subsistent, the essence of being and power.

To the Jews the name of God was the image of his being; God's nature shone in his name. They trembled before it as they had trembled before the Lord himself in Sinai. God speaks of his name as of himself. When he says of the Temple, "My name shall be there," he means by his name himself. In the mysterious book of the

Apocalypse he promises that those that come through tribulation shall be as pillars in the temple of God, and that he will write his name upon them; that is, that he will sanctify them and give them himself.

This is the sense in which we are to understand the commandment, "Thou shalt not take the Name of the Lord thy God in vain." This is how we are to understand the word in the prayer our Savior taught us, "Hallowed be thy name," and in the precept to begin whatever we undertake in God's name.

God's name is full of hidden power. It shadows forth the nature of infinitude, and the nature of him who is measureless plenitude and limitless sublimity.

In that name is also present what is deepest in us. There is a correspondence between God and our inmost being, for to God we inseparably belong. Created by God, for God, we are restless until we are wholly one with God. Our personalities have no other meaning or purpose than union with God in mutual love. Whatever nobility we possess, our soul's soul, is contained in the word God. He is my God, my source, my goal, the beginning and end of my being; him I worship, him I long for, him to whom with sorrow I confess my sins.

Strictly, all that exists is the name of God. Let us therefore beseech him not to take it in vain, but to hallow it. Let us ask him to make his name our light in glory. Let us not bandy it about meaninglessly. It is beyond price, thrice holy.

Let us honor God's name as we honor God himself. In reverencing God's name we reverence also the holiness of our own souls.

Sacred Signs, pages 101–106 (1929)

Selected Bibliography

Robert A. Krieg, CSC

I. Books by Romano Guardini published in English translation, listed in chronological order by the date of their original publication in German.

The Spirit of the Liturgy. Translated by Ada Lane. New York: Sheed and Ward, 1935. German publication: 1918.

The Church and the Catholic. Translated by Ada Lane. New York: Sheed and Ward, 1935. German publication: 1922.

Letters from Lake Como. Translated by Geoffrey W. Bromiley. Grand Rapids: William B. Eerdmans, 1994. German publication: 1927.

The Living God. Translated by Stanley Godman. New York: Pantheon Books, 1957. German publication: 1929.

Sacred Signs. Translated by Grace Branham. St. Louis: Pio Decimo, 1956. German publication: 1929.

The Lord's Prayer. Translated by Isabel McHugh. New York: Pantheon Books, 1958. German publication: 1932.

The Life of Faith. Translated by John Chapin. Westminster, MD: Newman, 1961. German publication: 1935.

Pascal for Our Time. Translated by Brian Thompson. New York: Herder and Herder, 1966. German publication: 1935.

The Lord. Translated by Elinor Castendyk Briefs. Chicago: Henry Regnery, 1954; new edition forthcoming. German publication: 1937.

Meditations Before Mass. Translated by Elinor Castendyk Briefs. Westminster, MD: Newman, 1955. Reprinted as *Preparing Yourself for Mass,* 1993. German publication: 1939.

Preparing Yourself for Mass. Translated by Elinor Castendyk Briefs. Mansfield, NH: Sophia Institute Press, 1993. Formerly *Meditations Before Mass,* 1955. German publication: 1939.

The World and the Person. Translated by Stella Lange. Chicago: Henry Regnery, 1965. German publication: 1939.

The Rosary of Our Lady. Translated by H. von Schuecking. New York: Kenedy, 1955. Reprinted: Mansfield, NH: Sophia Institute Press, 1994. German publication: 1940.

The Art of Praying. Translated by Leopold Loewenstein-Wertheim. Mansfield, NH: Sophia Institute Press, 1994. Formerly *Prayer in Practice,* 1957. German publication: 1943.

The Death of Socrates. Translated by Basil Wrighton. New York: Sheed and Ward, 1948. German publication: 1943.

Prayer in Practice. Translated by Leopold Loewenstein-Wertheim. New York: Pantheon, 1957. Reprinted as *The Art of Praying,* 1994. German publication: 1943.

Faith and the Modern Man. Translated by Charlotte E. Forsyth. New York: Pantheon Books, 1952. German publication: 1944.

Freedom, Grace and Destiny. Translated by John Murray. New York: Pantheon Books, 1961. German publication: 1948.

Prayers from Theology. Translated by Richard Newnham. New York: Herder and Herder, 1956. German publication: 1948.

The Word of God on Faith, Hope and Charity. Translated by Stella Lange. Chicago: Henry Regnery, 1963. German publication: 1949.

The End of the Modern World. Translated by Joseph Theman and Herbert Burke. New York: Sheed and Ward, 1956. German publication: 1950.

Power and Responsibility. Translated by Elinor Castendyk Briefs. Chicago: Henry Regnery, 1961. German publication: 1951.

Rilke's Duino Elegies. Translated by K. G. Knight. Chicago: Henry Regnery, 1961. German publication: 1953.

Jesus Christus: Meditations. Translated by Peter White. Chicago: Henry Regnery, 1959. German publication: 1957.

The Humanity of Christ. Translated by Ronald Walls. New York: Pantheon Books, 1964. German publication: 1958.

The Virtues. Translated by Stella Lange. Chicago: Henry Regnery, 1967. German publication: 1963.

The Wisdom of the Psalms. Translated by Stella Lange. Chicago: Henry Regnery, 1968. German publication: 1963.

The Church of the Lord. Translated by Stella Lange. Chicago: Henry Regnery, 1966. German publication: 1965.

II. Works about Romano Guardini and related works.

"Candid Monsignor." *Newsweek,* 45 10 January 1955, 50.

"Death of Romano Guardini." *Tablet* 222 (12 October 1968): 1021.

"Faith is the Center." *Time,* 75 14 March 1960, 51.

Balthasar, Hans Urs von. *Romano Guardini.* Translated by Albert Wimmer. San Francisco: Ignatius Press, forthcoming.

Berger, Teresa. "The Classical Liturgical Movement in Germany and Austria: Moved by Women?" *Worship* 66 (May 1992): 231–50.

Borghesi, Massimo. "Reflection: A New Beginning." *30 Days* 5 (1992): 62–68.

Dulles, Avery. *The Assurance of Things Hoped For.* New York: Oxford University Press, 1994, 130–32, passim.

Farrugia, Mario. "Romano Guardini (1885–1968)." In René Latourelle and Rino Fisichella (eds.), *Dictionary of Fundamental Theology,* 403–406. New York: Crossroad, 1995.

Hellwig, Monika K. "A Catholic Scholar's Journey Through the Twentieth Century." In *Faith and the Intellectual Life,* edited by James L. Heft, 71–85. Notre Dame: University of Notre Dame Press, 1966.

Hill, Roland. "Spiritual Liberator." *The Catholic World Report* 1 (June 1992): 52–55.

Krieg, Robert A. "Romano Guardini: Forerunner of Vatican II." *America* 169 (5 February 1993): 24–25.

———. "Romano Guardini: Paving the Way for Vatican II." *National Catholic Register* 70 (24 July 1994): 1, 9.

Krieg, Robert A., ed. *Romano Guardini: Proclaiming the Sacred in a Modern World.* Chicago: Liturgy Training Publications, 1995.

Kuehn, Regina. "Romano Guardini: Teacher of Teachers." In *How Firm A Foundation: Leaders of the Liturgical Movement,* edited by Robert Tuzik, 36–49. Chicago: Liturgy Training Publications, 1990.

Laubach, Jakob. "Romano Guardini." In *Theologians of Our Time,* edited by Leonhard Reinisch and translated by Charles H. Henkey, 109–26. Notre Dame: University of Notre Dame Press, 1964. The original German text appeared in 1960.

Misner, Paul. "Guardini, Romano." In *New Catholic Encyclopedia,* 16: Supplement 1967–1974, edited by David Eggenberger, 198–99. Washington, DC: Publishers Guild, Inc. with McGraw-Hill Book Company, 1974.

Rahner, Karl. "Romano Guardini's Successor." In *I Remember,* translated by Harvey D. Egan, 73–75. New York: Crossroad, 1985.

———. "Thinker and Christian: Obituary of Romano Guardini." In *Opportunities for Faith,* translated by Edward Quinn, 127–31. New York: The Seabury Press, 1975. The original German text appeared in 1968.

Ratzinger, Joseph. "Guardini on Christ in Our Century." *Crisis* 14 (1996): 14–15.

Schoof, T. Mark. *A Survey of Catholic Theology 1800–1970.* Translated by N. D. Smith, 81–84, passim. New York: Paulist Newman Press, 1970.

III. The excerpts of Romano Guardini's works in this book are used with the permission of the copyright holders of these editions.

The Church and the Catholic and *The Spirit of the Liturgy* (one volume). Translated by Ada Lane. © 1935, Sheed & Ward, New York.

The Faith and Modern Man. Translated by Charlotte E. Forsyth. © 1953, Burns & Oates, London.

The Lord. Translated by Elinor Castendyk Briefs. © 1954, Henry Regnery Company, Chicago. All rights reserved. Reprinted by special permission of Regnery Publishing Inc., Washington DC.

The End of the Modern World: A Search for Orientation. Translated by Joseph Theman and Herbert Burke. © 1956, Sheed & Ward, New York.

Freedom, Grace, and Destiny: Three Chapters in the Interpretation of Existence. Translated by John Murray, sj. © 1961, Pantheon Books, a division of Random House, Inc. Regnery Logos Edition 1965.

Power and Responsibility: A Course of Action for the New Age. Translated by Elinor Castendyk Briefs. © 1961, Henry Regnery Company, Chicago. All rights reserved. Reprinted by special permission of Regnery Publishing Inc., Washington DC.

The Church of the Lord: On the Nature and Mission of the Church. Translated by Stella Lange. © 1966, Henry Regnery Company, Chicago. All rights reserved. Reprinted by special permission of Regnery Publishing Inc., Washington DC.

Sacred Signs. Translated by Grace Branham. © 1979, Michael Glazier, Inc., Wilmington DE, on behalf of the estate of David Dunne.

Meditations Before Mass, (now published as *Preparing Yourself for Mass*). Translated by Elinor Castendyk Briefs. © 1993, Sophia Institute Press, Manchester NH.

Letters from Lake Como: Explorations in Technology and the Human Race. With an introduction by Louis Dupré. Translated by Geoffrey W. Bromiley. © 1994, Wm. Eerdmans Publishing Company, Grand Rapids MI.

Index

Adoration, practice of, 93 – 96
Aging process, and stages of faith, 85 – 93
Altar, symbolism of, 134, 157–160
Anxiety, growth of in society, 50, 57– 58
Apocalypse, 101, 102, 116
Apostles, 66 – 67, 68, 69, 98 – 99, 103 – 8, 114
Asceticism, importance of, 42 – 44
Augustine, Saint, 61, 160

Beatitudes. *See* Sermon on the Mount
Blessing, act of, 170 –171
Bonaventure, Saint, 3, 5

Candles, symbolism of, 165 – 66
Catholic Center Party (Germany), 5, 6
Church
    beginnings of, 98 –115
    characteristics of, 116 – 29, 132 – 46
Church and the Catholic, The, excerpts from, 120 – 29
Church of the Lord, The, excerpts from, 103 – 8, 108 –13, 113 –15, 116 –18, 119 – 20
Communalism
    in the church, 75, 99 –101, 123 – 26, 132 – 40
    in society, 16 –17, 30, 48 – 49, 124 – 25, 128
    See also Individuality and autonomy
Confession, 134
Contemplation and solitude, importance of, 40 – 42, 55 – 57, 133 – 34
Creative impulse, 18 – 20, 22, 23, 72, 149 – 52

Death, meaning of, 73 –74, 91– 93, 141 – 42, 172 –73
Demons, 52 – 53

End of the Modern World, excerpts from, 14, 15 –18, 26 – 28, 50 – 56, 57– 58
Ethical norms, decline of, 24 – 26, 53 – 54, 55
Eucharist, 79 – 84, 99, 133, 168 –70

Faith, challenges of, 66 –76, 85 – 93
Faith and Modern Man, The, excerpts from, 85 – 88, 89 – 93, 93 – 96
Fellowship. *See* Communalism
Freedom, Grace, and Destiny, excerpts from, 55 – 57, 58 – 64

Goethe, Johann Wolfgang von, 54
Grace, 62–64, 101, 150
Guardini, Romano, life of, 1–10

Heresies, 145
Herwegen, Ildefons, 4–5
History, dynamics of, 14–15, 18, 20–22, 26, 28–32, 33–40, 44–50, 50–64, 91, 112, 119, 128–29
Hitler, Adolf, 6. *See also* Nazi regime
Holy Spirit, 101, 103–8, 111, 114, 119, 120, 123, 151
Holy water, symbolism of, 167–69
Hours, consecrated, 143, 171–74
Humanity, nature of, 20–24, 143
Humility, importance of, 37, 137

Ignatius of Antioch, Saint, 169
Incarnation, 62–64, 66–68
Individuality and autonomy
    in the church, 72–2, 100–1, 123–29, 132–40
    in society, 16–17, 23–24, 26, 27–31, 53–54
    See also Communalism

Jerusalem, 101
Jesus Christ
    and beginnings of the church, 79–84, 98–113
    central message of, 70–79
    as church, 113–15, 117–18, 120–23, 136
    and Incarnation, 62–64, 66–68, 89
John the Evangelist, Saint, 67, 108, 113, 118, 158, 160
Juventus, 3–4

Kierkegaard, Soren, 119
Kuhn, Helmut, 4

Leadership, new requirements of, 33–43
Letters from Lake Como, excerpt from, 43–49
Liturgy
    characteristics of, 132–41, 147–54
    elements of, 157–77
    history of, 143–47
    symbolism of, 155–57
Lord, The, excerpts from, 66–84, 98–103
Lord's Prayer, the, 100

Marriage and family, 22, 25, 42–43, 71, 102, 170–71
Mary, Virgin, 67, 134, 143, 174
Meditations Before Mass, excerpts from, 132–36, 157–60, 163–64
Middle Ages, 18, 21, 24, 30, 50, 53. See also History, dynamics of

Modern era, end of. *See* History, dynamics of
Moses, 79 – 82, 105, 176

Nature, ideas about, 16 –17, 19, 25, 26 – 28, 31, 37– 40, 48, 51– 52, 54
Nazi regime, 4, 6, 8 – 9, 24 – 25, 35, 54 – 55
New era, beginning of. *See* History, dynamics of
Nietzsche, Friedrich, 170
Non-Christian religions, 31, 74, 76
Nuclear threat, 15, 17–18, 33 – 34

Paradise, idea of, 62 – 63, 175 –76
Pascal, Blaise, 61
Pasch (Passover), 79 – 84
Paul, Saint, 64, 75, 77, 80, 93 –100, 101, 102, 107– 8, 109 –10, 116, 134 – 5, 160
Pentecost, 99, 103 –109, 114, 119, 121
Peter, Saint, 86, 98 – 99, 104, 106, 108, 134
Postures and gestures, during liturgy, 95, 161– 64
Power, 37, 79
    attitudes toward, 14 –15
    communal forms of, 16 –17, 30, 126 – 27, 128
    in religious sense, 110 –111, 170 –171
    and technology, 16 –17, 27– 32
    See also Leadership, new requirements of
Power and Responsibility, excerpts from, 14 –15, 18 – 26, 28 – 43
Prayer, 100, 140 – 42, 145 – 46

Quickborn movement, 4, 6 – 8

Rahner, Karl, 9
Revelation, 36, 61– 63, 67–73, 83 – 84, 113, 117–18, 141
Rousseau, Jean-Jacques, 51

Sacred Signs, excerpts from, 160 – 63, 164 –77
Science. *See* Technology
Scriptures, 57– 58, 114, 119 – 20, 141, 143
Sermon on the Mount, 76 –79, 100
Sign of the cross, symbolism of, 156, 160 – 61
Spirit of the Liturgy, excerpts from, 136 – 46, 147– 54, 155 – 57

Technology
    ascendancy of, 16 – 20, 22 – 23, 26 – 28, 44 – 45
    and religion, 17–18, 24 – 26, 45 – 46

Vatican II, 10